**INSIDER TIP** Stroll and shop

On Fridays and Saturdays Marina Walk turns into an open-air market. Yachts, views of extraordinary buildings and people from all over the world make the shopping a pleasant excuse to stroll here → **p. 43**

**INSIDER TIP** Dance on the Palm Jumeirah

Sanctuary is the name of the superclub in the gigantic themed Atlantis hotel. Every wish is fulfilled in an area designated specially for live entertainment, a lounge area and an open-air terrace with a view of the Arabian Gulf and the Palm Jumeirah → **p. 71**

**INSIDER TIP** Back to school

The beginnings of school education in Dubai: the historic Al-Ahmadiya School for boys has been restored, and the old classrooms have been furnished as in former days and peopled with life-size figures of pupils → **p. 32**

**INSIDER TIP** View from above

A trip across the Palm Jumeirah to the Hotel Atlantis on the elevated monorail gives you a great view of luxury villas and hotels on this manmade island (photo below) → **p. 44**

**INSIDER TIP** Organic and delicious

Try something that tastes good and is healthy in the Organic Foods and Café in Dubai Mall: fair-trade chocolate, biscuits with green credentials and organically grown fruit. The only ecologically sound address in the whole mall → **p. 51**

**INSIDER TIP** Cable car but no mountains

In the large Creekside Park locals and Indian families glide through the air along the Creek: with a view of the water, the boats and the yachts → **p. 29**

**INSIDER TIP** Teatime view

Even a cup of Earl Grey makes you feel high at 200 m above sea level – in the Skyview Bar of the Burj Al Arab hotel tower → **p. 51**

# BEST OF ...

**FOR FREE**

● **Fountain display at the Burj Khalifa**
The Dubai Fountain at twilight: classical music and specially composed works accompany an ingenious light show and enormous jets of water rhythmically spurting up to 150 m high → p. 37

● **Movies under the stars**
The 'Russell Crowe Night' or the 'Hilary Swank Night' – something for every cinematic taste can be seen on Sunday evenings on the roof terrace of the Wafi Mall. Seating on the big beanbags is free, the drinks at the bar have to be paid for → p. 73

● **Aquarium XXL**
The Dubai Aquarium in the Dubai Mall extends over three floors. A panoramic window 8 x 4 m in size gives you a view of rays, sharks and tropical fish (photo) → pp. 62, 88

● **City tour with shoppers**
Dubai is a big place and the shopping malls are not close together – which gives you the opportunity to take a tour on the shuttle bus of the Deira City Centre shopping mall and see the city from a different angle. It picks up shoppers from their hotels and takes them back again → p. 61

● **Culture with the locals**
When the sun goes down, guest workers and natives of Dubai come to the Heritage & Diving Village to see how their traditions are presented. These two open-air museums sitting side by side in a beautiful location on the Creek invite visitors to look at the stands and little workshops → p. 30

● **Al-Ahmadiya School**
In this historic former school for boys, citizens of the Emirate once learned to read and write. A visit to the school with its courtyard and galleries is free of charge → p. 32

○○○○ Dots in guidebook refer to 'Best of ...' tips

● *Weekend in the desert*
In the desert resort of Bab al-Shams, the 'gateway to the sun', guests live amongst the sand dunes. For a few days you can become a modern Bedouin – with the luxury typical of Dubai and old Arab architectural traditions → **p. 20**

● *Dinner on a dhow*
Old Arabian trading ships as floating restaurants: the romantic sunset dhow trip lasts about two hours. As the last rays of the sun fall on the city, help yourself from the buffet and see Dubai from the water → **p. 72**

● *Dubai Shopping Festival*
A four-week shopping spree: discounts, prize draws with millions to be won, fashion shows, charity galas and other events are the highlights of this glamorous festival → **p. 91**

● *Jumeirah Beach*
Wealthy locals flock to these miles of long sandy beach with Dubai's emblem, the Burj Al Arab, the offshore man-made island Palm Jumeirah and the Rooftop Bar of the Royal Mirage Hotel, a trendy rendezvous in the evening (photo) → **p. 40**

● *Bastakiya*
Dubai's most authentic quarter gets its character from narrow alleys, some of them shaded by palm-frond roofs, and merchants› houses that are now occupied by galleries, restaurants and cafés → **p. 28**

● *Marina with skyscrapers*
Dubai Marina, a district of the city that is really buzzing, can easily be explored on foot: spectacular skyscrapers, chic cafés, the best-known night clubs and the huge artificially made marina with its yachts and sailing boats → **p. 42**

● *Get to the top*
Burj Khalifa is the world›s tallest building. For a special thrill pay a visit to 'At the Top', the viewing platform with an outdoor terrace on the 124th floor. This organised one-hour tour places Dubai at your feet from a height of 1450 ft → **p. 37**

ONLY IN

# BEST OF ...

### ● *Underground in the Dubai Museum*
On the lower floor of the Al-Fahidi Fort you are in semi-darkness, and it›s a pleasantly cool place to learn about everyday life in the Gulf in bygone days → **p. 30**

### ● *Oriental open sesame*
When the temperature gets to about 40 degrees (°F 104) and things slow down in the Spice Souk and Gold Souk, enjoy the bazaar atmosphere in the air-conditioned lanes of the Souk Al-Bahar and the Souk Khan Murjan → **p. 65**

### ● *Chill out in the ice bar*
Seats, tables, walls and the bar itself – in the Chillout Bar everything is made of ice. For protection against the sudden fall in temperature – you go from the outdoor heat to rooms cooled to minus six degrees (°F minus 21) – guests are given a padded jacket, scarf and gloves in the acclimatisation room → **p. 68**

### ● *Shopping and more*
The Dubai Mall houses not only hundreds of boutiques, but also an ice rink, an aquarium, cinemas and indoor theme parks – all air-conditioned → **p. 38**

### ● *Dubai by rail*
A cool and cheap city tour. As the Metro only goes underground in the city centre and is a high-level railway outside the centre, you get a good view of Dubai as you cross it in about one hour (photo) → **p. 97**

### ● *Downhill or armchair skiing...*
At Ski Dubai new snow falls every night to replenish the slopes. If downhill skiing is not your thing, you can slide down the slope in a tube. The lazy alternative is to watch the action through the panorama windows of Café Moritz while sipping hot tea, chocolate or coffee by the fireplace → **p. 45**

HEAT

# RELAX AND CHILL OUT
## Take it easy and spoil yourself

● *Shisha with a view*
The Apple Café & Restaurant is a wonderful place for a relaxed break from shopping: prices are low, and the fruit cocktails (mocktails) and shishas with apple aroma go down well with a spectacular view of Dubai Creek → **p. 57**

● *In the hammam*
Flower essences, mosaics and tall domes – the hammam in the Arabian Court of the One&Only Royal Mirage is a fairy-tale world where you can enjoy the threefold relaxations of sweating out some toxins, a Moroccan massage and cooling off in the jacuzzi → **p. 78**

● *Dinner on the pier*
After sundown, thousands of little lanterns illuminate the wind towers and palatial hotels of Madinat Jumeirah. The best spot at this time is the Pierchic restaurant, where you can admire the scenery from a wooden pier on the sea front → **p. 53**

● *Gamelan music and Balinese oils*
Small but perfect: in the Ritz Carlton Hotel therapists trained in Bali and Thailand spoil stressed-out guests with treatments that indulge body and soul → **p. 21**

● *Sunbathe on the Arabian Gulf*
Dubai expats and visitors whose hotels are not close to the beach like to relax in the Jumeirah Beach Park. For a modest price you have access to little beach coves, sunshades and showers → **p. 42**

● *A night at the Hatta Fort Hotel*
The only thing that could disturb you here is the chirping of birds: around 65 miles from Dubai, close to the traditional settlement of Hatta and nestling in wonderful gardens, this is a summer oasis for residents of Dubai. With a view of the bare Hajar Mountains they enjoy an abundance of natural peace and quiet (photo) → **p. 46**

INTRODUCTION

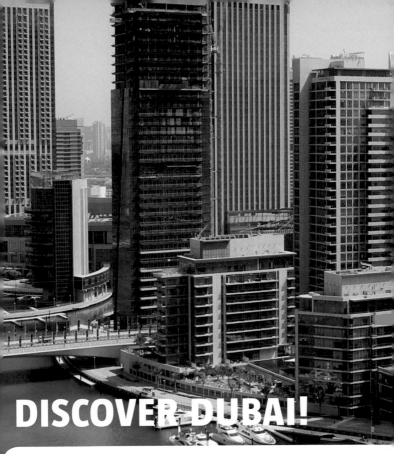

# DISCOVER DUBAI!

Dubai – you have to see it for yourself. Spectacular luxury hotels, mega-malls for shoppers and utopian construction projects have turned an Arabian trading port on the Creek into a global village measured in superlatives. The world's tallest building and largest man made waterway, artificial islands that are visible from space, the biggest airport – unparalleled construction projects are announced all the time and carried out in no time at all. Whole new city districts surrounded by lakes and marina have been built on the sand, with a transport infrastructure of multi-lane highways flanked by skyscrapers with mirror façades.

The opening of the seven-star Burj Al Arab hotel in 1999 was just the beginning; within a few years Dubai became a sought-after destination for short breaks, the eighth wonder of the world at the start of the 21st century. The emirate, which is ruled by a sheikh, drew visitors to the Arabian Gulf like a magnet with sunshine, beaches and the invention of awe-inspiring sights. Seen from the observation deck of the 2716-ft Burj Khalifa a sea of houses stretches to the horizon. From up there even

Photo: Dubai Marina

the nearby skyscrapers seem like cute toy houses. At the foot of this tower, the most prestigious place to live in Dubai, a residential settlement was built in the traditional Arabian style. Alongside villas that look like historic desert palaces, the old-world Souk Al-Bahar and an opulent hotel, The Palace of the Old Town, there are also attractions such as a man-made lake and the astounding jets of the Dubai Fountain.

Dubai is pushing back the desert further and further. 16 miles from the city centre, the Dubai Marina is a spectacular new district that boasts a huge man-made marina and (when it is finished) about 200 high-rises with out-of-the-ordinary architecture. One reason for the rapid development of this mega-city is that the oil reserves are being depleted. In 15 to 40 years, it is forecast, no more oil will be extracted in Dubai. As a centre of finance and commerce, Dubai is taking precautions and opening up new sources of income such as international tourism, which already bring the emirate more than 25 per cent of its revenue. Sunshine all year round and clean, light-coloured sand make a beach holiday in the Emirate a pleasure for many. Add to that 40 large shopping malls with goods from all over the world at moderate prices. Uninterrupted growth and the realisation of crazy-sounding visions following the motto ‚nothing is impossible' was the ever-present mantra in the emirate. Nowhere else in the world is such a large number of attention-grabbing construction projects being carried out.

A gigantic residential project, Dubai-style: the Palm Jumeirah

But Dubai also polarises opinion: while some people see it as the most modern and vibrant city anywhere and are intoxicated by the dizzying speed of its development, others are put off by its excess and feel that the extravagant luxury and consumption that is normal here are ostentatious and trivial. If you speak to the foreigners who live in Dubai, you get a different picture. In their judgement the most important things are not the size and superlatives behind the frenzied growth in Dubai, but the quality of life that is on offer in this emirate on the Arabian Gulf. Now that the economic and financial crisis of Dubai has largely been overcome, Europeans who work here are once again enjoying the enormous opportunities that are available to them: the dynamic life of the sheikhdoms, the countless leisure facilities – and the permanent sunshine. They say you can get used to the summer months, when it is as hot as hell, the water in swimming pools has to be cooled, the city heats up like a huge oven and public life becomes more and more lethargic: ‚We simply

> **In summer the pool water has to be cooled**

compare the temperatures over 40° C (104° F), which make it impossible to live outdoors, with the icy winter months in Europe. When it's freezing, we don't want to leave the house either.' It depends how you look at it: at the start of the cooler winter months, when the thermometer falls below 30° C (104° F) again, the latest winter collections are displayed in the boutiques and shopping malls, and fashion-conscious

women kit themselves out with woollen skirts and boots in air-conditioned buildings. On winter evenings the temperature can fall dramatically in this region, and then it pays to have a pullover.

At almost 3900 km² (2440 sq mi), the second-largest of the seven emirates that make up the United Arab Emirates (CAE), is about as large as Mallorca. As most of the emirate, which extends approximately 45 miles inland, consists of desert, over 95 per cent of its 1.7 million inhabitants live in Dubai City and its surroundings. (The United Arab Emirates are described in detail in a separate MARCO POLO guide.)

Dubai has changed by holding its finger on the fast-forward button. A huge construction boom drives the dynamic economy and brings in people from all corners of the world. The real estate and service sectors have been growing for years. 'Only a very small part of my visions for Dubai have been realised',

Sheikh Mohammed Bin Rashid al-Maktoum, head of government and the most important stakeholder in the emirate, is reported to have said. As recently as the 1960s Dubai was an insignificant Bedouin settlement by the sea that had a population of

a few thousand people living from oasis agriculture and fishing. The region's meteoric rise began with the discovery and export of oil. The ruling Al-Maktoum family gave the native population a generous share of the new affluence. Young couples are given a house and land as well as an interest-free loan. The Dubai people have unique facilities for education and training. The state pays for health care and pensions, which is probably the main reason for the political stability of the emirate and for the fact that the population are happy with their standard of living, one of the world's highest, even though they have no political influence.

The locals also have to live with the fact that they have become a minority. Only 10 per cent of the residents of Dubai are nationals or locals and can benefit from the financial advantages granted by the state. 90 per cent or residents are foreigners, usually expatriates with a fixed-term contract of employment. They represent 120 different nationalities. Everybody has to abide by the local laws. Drink-driving, for example, leads not merely to the loss of the driving licence and several days or even months in prison, but sometimes to deportation. Despite liberal attitudes in Dubai, Islamic values and laws apply still here in the 21st century. 'Allah u Akbar' – five times a day the muezzin calls the faithful to prayer from the minarets of the mosques. When darkness falls, thousands of lights make the Jumeirah Mosque look like a building from the distant past, even though it is only 30 years old. Record-breaking, luxury and the desire for profit are only one side of the emirate. While champagne flows in the bars and clubs and the fashionable rich party in locations that get ever more spectacular, the people of Dubai live according to the rules of an Islamic state. The Koran is not only the basis of justice but also dominates everyday and family life. Local women are expected not to go out alone at night, to wear a long black robe in public and cover their hair. During Ramadan, the annual month of fasting, all public life slows down. And the life of Arab people continues to revolve around the extended family.

Dubai is growing without any restrictions: faster and faster, higher and higher, bigger and bigger. The Burj Khalifa with its over 2600 ft had not even been finished

when Dubai announced the construction of a building that would exceed the 1000-m mark – we are talking 3200 ft! Until recently such energy-intensive prestige projects were more important for Dubai than a careful use of resources. And so the emirate became the

world's biggest waster of energy. Reports about this in international media have had an effect: Dubai increasingly plans to consider ecology. Since 2008 it has made a commitment to complying with its own environmental guidelines by saving water and resources, by recycling and by favouring renewable energy sources. However, it remains to be seen whether this 'green construction' is more than a marketing gimmick. An awareness of ecological issues is still absent. The locals love luxury and technology above all else, and the guest workers from Asia who want to raise their

Prestige architecture: the Burj Khalifa, the world's tallest building at 2716 feet

low standard of living are scarcely in a position to concern themselves with sustainability. There are only sporadic signs of a change in thinking. It is often the Western expatriates in the emirate who set a good example by saving electricity, turning down the air conditioning, taking a bag with them when they go shopping and asking for organic products.

Understatement is not the order of the day in Dubai. Nevertheless, during the international financial crisis the prices for luxury properties fell even here. Ambitious building projects were halted, façades with nothing behind them can be seen all over the city. In mid-2010, however, the end of the crisis was officially announced: the indebted Dubai World state company plans to pay back its borrowings of 14.4 billion US$ by 2018, partly by selling some of its real estate. The markets recovered after this plan was made public. Dubai, described as the 'bankrupt sheikhdom' in western media at the peak of the financial crisis, seems to have made adjustments and is forging ahead again. Anyone who visits Dubai will notice that the optimism has returned.

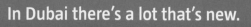

# In Dubai there's a lot that's new.
# A few of the most interesting are listed below

## **1** Contemporary style

*Homemade* Local artists like *Hind Mezaina (www.hind-mezaina.com)* or *Lateefa bint Maktoum (www.lateefabint-maktoum.com)* are now getting the attention that they deserve in their home country too. To see exhibitions by up-and-coming creative people, go to the innovative *thejamjar* gallery *(17a Street, Comm 368, www.the jamjardubai.com, photo)* or the trendy *Courtyard Gallery & Café (Street 6, corner of Sheikh Zayed Road/Al Manara Road, www.courtyardgallerydubai.com).*

## Sand instead of snow **2**

*Dune sports* Boarders can have a great time here even without snow. Apart from the popular red dune *(Big Red)*, many other sandy summits in the emirate attract practitioners of extreme sports. But these dunes shift. The best dunes for boarders are known at *City Smart (www.citysmart.ae)*. *Desert Road Tours* also runs sand-boarding trips – and teaches beginners how to get up speed *(Al-Khor Plaza, 5th Floor, Office 503, www.desertroad tours.com).*

## Above the clouds

**3**

*Dizzying* A twinkling sea of lights at your feet and a cool drink in your hand. Dubai's skylounges are the perfect locations for falling in love with the emirate. In the spectacular *Neo* bar *(in The Address hotel, Burj Dubai Boulevard, photo)* you can lose your heart just as quickly as on the roof terrace of the *One&Only Royal Mirage* hotel with its overwhelming view *(The Roof Top Bar, Al Sufouh Road)*. *360°* makes it even easier. This building rotates on its own axis to save you turning your head *(in the Jumeirah Beach Hotel, Jumeirah Road)*.

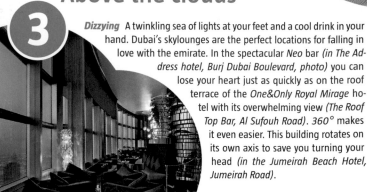

# Fabulous fashion

*Fashion from the emirate* The work of local designers almost seems like a tropical garden. The dominant colours are lemon yellow, garish green and pink, with artistic embroidery and applications added on – sometimes with tongue in cheek. Precious, flowing fabrics and intoxicating colours are the trademark of *Royal Rickshaw* (www.royalrickshaw.com). Their creations can be found at *Tiger Lily* in the *Wafi Mall (Oud Metha Road)*. Look for the accessories to match at *Pink Sushi (fashion.pink-sushi.com)* or in the cool concept store *Fivegreen (Oud Metha Road, www.fivegreen. com)*. The annual *Dubai Fashion Week (www.dfw.ae, photo)* provides a good impression of the fashion scene in the little emirate.

# A good conscience

*A good deed* *Backstage* not only puts on excellent performances; this non-profit theatre group also takes care of the next generation with talent, sometimes casting directly from the street. See the results in the *Shelter (Warehouse 209, 318 Road, www.shelter.ae)*. The *Al Noor Centre* is an organisation that helps mentally or physically handicapped children, or those with learning difficulties and behavioural problems. All those who kick a ball or swing a racquet in its sports hall are doing good for others as well as themselves – the income benefits the kids supported by *Al-Noor (Al Barsha, www. alnoorspneeds.ae)*. The *Holistic Institute* where meditation courses, art events and exhibitions are held *(Jumeirah Lake Towers, www. theholisticinstitute.org, photo)* is financed entirely by donations.

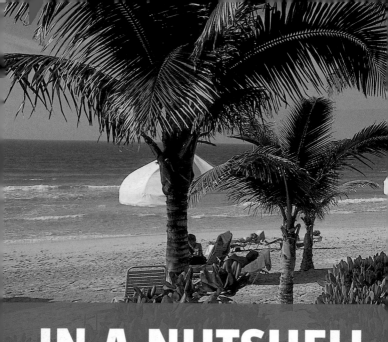

# IN A NUTSHELL

## BEACH LIFE

The hotels along Jumeirah Beach have private beaches, and they really are private: only for hotel residents! City hotels (i.e. without a beach) in the five-star category (and some with four stars) have the hotel's own beach club for guests with a shuttle transfer. Tourists without such access to the beach have only one option really: to go to a public beach *(beach park)* such as the Jumeirah Beach Park or the Al-Mamzar Beach Park *(see p. 42)*. For a few dirhams you can have sunshades, loungers, toilets, cafés and peace and quiet. The second option, an open beach without any charges and with no infrastructure, cannot really be recommended: those who swim or sunbathe there are stared at, even besieged, by expatriates from Pakistan, India and other countries; the police regularly chase up these people and issue warnings for nuisance.

## CALLIGRAPHY

Lettering as an encounter with the transcendental, developed into a high art over the course of centuries: calligraphy, the art of 'beautiful writing' is regarded as being  − after architecture − the most significant Islamic contribution to art. Harmony between the spoken and the written word was the aim, evolving from the responsibility to write down the words of the Prophet − in a society that already put the highest possible value on spoken poetry. This form of art originated with the birth of Islam,

Photo: Jumeirah Beach near the Royal Mirage Hotel

## Oil, falcons & desert – take a look at what's characteristic, remarkable and special about this mega-city

and today it is still mainly concerned with the verses of the Koran, which are portrayed in calligraphic form. Two letters of the word 'Allah', namely 'Alif' and 'Lam', became the focal points of calligraphic work. Each year in February an exhibition of calligraphy is held in Dubai. Further examples can be seen in Dubai's art galleries and in the Jumeirah Mosque, modern calligraphy in the Art Space Gallery *(www.artspace-dubai. com)*, and calligraphy can be bought to take home from the artist Majid Roum-

mah *(www.roummah.com)* in Madinat Jumeirah. In the neighbouring emirate of Sharjah there is even a museum of calligraphy.

## CHARITY

When people go to Dubai for trade fairs, usually the luxury goods and consumer goods segments are involved. In addition to this, for over ten years now the emirate has organised the International Humanitarian Aid and Development Fair *(DIHAD)* taking place in April.

# FALCONS

Not dogs and cats but camels and falcons are the favourite animals of the people of Dubai. The birds of prey are trained for several months by experienced falconers. When the bird has got used to humans and knows what it has to do, it goes to a new owner. Out in the desert a falcon will take off from an outstretched arm and plummet down when it has seen its prey, waiting there motionless for its master. The most valuable falcons have a price tag of up to 1 million dirham and sometimes accompany their owners abroad for hunting. Hunting with falcons is an ancient passion of the Arabs that foreigners rarely get to see. The only places where trained falcons are shown are the desert hotels of Al-Maha and ● Bab al-Shams, and sometimes they can be seen at an organised ‚Bedouin dinner'.

# HENNA

To this day hands and feet painted with complex patterns in henna paste are part of the ideal of beauty for an Arabian woman. The powder that is made from the leaves of the henna plant is mixed with aromatic oils and limejuice to make a paste that is applied to the skin. The red-brown colouring lasts for several weeks before fading. In Dubai a range of beauty salons offer this henna decoration to tourists.

# LUXURY CARS

Nowhere in the world are high-value limousines as thick on the ground as in the emirate. At weekends Hummers, Porsches and Maybachs queue up outside the foyers of luxury hotels for valet parking. The object of desire of the Dubai rich is the Bugatti Veyron, the most expensive and the fastest sports car in the world built in series produc-

Traditional adornment of the hands: a henna tattoo

In collaboration with the United Nations and the International Red Cross, thousands of participants from about 20 countries meet each year at this fair for conferences, workshops and discussions concerned with humanitarian aid in areas affected by catastrophes, developing countries and charitable projects. Dubai Cares *(www.dubaicares.ae)* is a state organisation with the stated aim of enabling every child on earth to attend school. It builds schools and libraries, for example in Africa and Asia, and arranges meals for schoolchildren.

tion, which costs over a million dollars. It is a racing car licensed for normal road traffic, has over 1001 HP and can reach speeds above 400 km/h. One in five of these Bugattis is registered in the UAE. In Dubai the automobile makers have their largest and most extravagantly designed showrooms. BMW, for example, promotes its 7 series and the X5 and X6 4 x 4 models with most success, getting a lot of orders from Dubai nationals. Bargaining over the price is a matter of course in Dubai – whether it's a limousine or a high-class racing camel.

# OIL

Millions of years ago a layer of mud formed in the oceans from animals that died and sank to the bottom. For lack of oxygen they did not decompose but were transformed into liquid hydrocarbons. Movements in the earth's surface pushed mountains over these hydrocarbons and forced them through the porous layers of clay and sediment that lay beneath into enormous cavities that were surrounded by impermeable rock. These reserves of oil now lie in a partly ran-

# RELAX & ENJOY

Trained therapists from Indonesia or Thailand, beauty products from all over the world: in addition to many excellent spas in the big hotels the number of day spas is increasing all the time.

### Lime Spa at the Desert Palm Hotel (115 D4) (𝄐 0)
Dubai's classiest spa is in a boutique hotel that puts the emphasis on nature and understatement. Customised treatments, products by the French company Anne Sémon, which uses natural ingredients and aromatherapy. *Daily 10am–8pm | treatments from 495 Dh | Desert Palm Resort & Spa | Al-Awir Road (E44, 12 mi east of Dubai) | tel. 04 3 23 88 88 | www.desertpalm.ae*

### Spa at the Ritz-Carlton-Hotel ● (102 B1) (𝄐 J3)
Gentle Balinese oil massage and other treatments from the island of the gods in an exotic atmosphere. Try the Javanese body scrub, then relax in the outdoor pool with lotus flowers and bam-

boo. *Daily 9am–8pm | massages from 265 Dh | Ritz-Carlton | Al-Sufouh Road | tel. 04 3 18 61 84 | www.ritzcarlton.com/en/Properties/Dubai/Spa | Metro Red Line: Dubai Marina*

### Sensasia Urban Spa (107 E1) (𝄐 T4)
A young hip clientele likes this spa, which was designed in a minimalist Asian style. The most popular treatments here are hot-stone massage and coffee peeling. *Daily 10am–10pm | massage from 295 Dh | The Village Mall, 1st floor | Jumeirah Beach Road | tel. 04 3 49 88 50 | www.sensasiaspas.com | Metro Red Line: Emirates Towers*

### Cleopatra Spa (108 B5) (𝄐 U6)
Dubai's biggest and most famous day spa, divided into female and male spas. Oil treatments from Bali, reiki and much more. *Daily 8.30am (men 9.30) to 10pm | treatments from 195 Dh | Wafi Centre | Oud Metha Road | tel. 04 3 24 77 00 | www.wafi.com | Metro Green Line: Healthcare City*

dom distribution under the surface of the earth – with a concentration around the Arabian Gulf. This is where the oil is now flowing. Abu Dhabi, Iran, Iraq and Kuwait each have reserves of more than 100 billion barrels (1 barrel is about 160 litres), and Saudi Arabia has twice as much.

# POLITICS

The government of the UAE is composed of the council of rulers (the emir is the *ruler)* of the seven emirates. They nominate the members of the cabinet and National Assembly. The president is the Emir of Abu Dhabi (Sheikh Khalifa Bin Zayed al-Nahyan). His deputy and prime minister is the ruler of Dubai (Sheikh Mohammed Bin Rashid al-Maktoum). In this feudal-style system of government it is usually the eldest son who inherits the title. In 2004, for example, in Abu Dhabi the position passed from Sheikh Zayed, the first president of the country, to his son (= Bin) Khalifa.

# POPULATION

Of the 1.7 million residents of Dubai, only 10 % are locals (or *nationals)*; i.e. the great majority are foreigners *(expatriates)* who have come to live and work in Dubai. The emirates prefer to give employment to Muslims, which is why many Pakistanis work on construction sites or drive taxis. Nannies often come from Malaysia, but are also recruited from Sri Lanka and the Philippines. Employees in commercial functions are frequently Indians and Egyptians, and staff in the hotel business are very international.

In Dubai many more men are to be seen than women. The reason for this is that the men who work for low wages in the construction industry receive no residence permit for their families. They get basic accommodation in dormitories and usually an air ticket for four weeks' annual leave at home.

# RAIN

By Dubai standards, rubber boots are an eccentric form of footwear: the sun shines about 360 days per year. On the remaining five days when it rains there is chaos: cars form tailbacks miles long and the city is gridlocked. The next day it is then reported that 'Heavy rain led to traffic chaos yesterday.' As the roads are not equipped for the torrential rain that sometimes falls and the emirate only has a rudimentary drainage system, the water cannot run off and its level rises. Everywhere you look tankers are in operation to pump off the water. And soon after the sun shines again.

# SHEIKH & EMIR

'Sheikh' is an honorific title traditionally given to the spiritual head of an Arabian Bedouin tribe. As a spiritual master the sheikh is ideally part of an unbroken line in oral tradition that goes back to the Prophet Mohammed and thus to the 'wisdom of the heart'. Thus it is easy to understand why some Arabian sheikhs are accorded great devotion long after their death, in contrast to an emir, who is entitled to rule and to command a company of soldiers (in Arabic 'amir' means 'commander'). In Dubai today the term 'sheikh' is also the official title of the head of government. In personal conversations, the correct respectful way to refer to Sheikh Mohammed is 'His Highness'.

# SHISHAS

Strawberry, banana or latte macchiato? The kinds of tobacco smoked in shisha cafés change according to the season. Even though word has now got around that smoking is bad for your health, in recent years more and more establishment where a shisha, or water-cooled pipe, can be ordered have sprung up. And what used to be the preserve of Bedouin and men is now increasingly finding favour with women. Usually it is foreign women who indulge in an aromatic smoke in public and enjoy the relaxing bubbling sound of the pipe – which is, after all, also known as a *hubbly-bubbly* – as an essential part of chilling out. As a low-cost souvenir, too, shishas can be found everywhere in Dubai. The cheapest ones are in the shops of the Old Souk in Deira.

## WASTE

Dubai is clean and no rubbish lies around on the streets, and no empty bottles or cans are thrown onto the ground. This is somewhat surprising in view of the fact that a large proportion of expatriates come from India and Pakistan, countries where it is unfortunately normal to dump rubbish on the streets. The government of Dubai found the solution by threatening fines: little bilingual signs warn of a 'littering fee 500 Dh' which is charged to anyone found throwing away litter.

## WATER & DESERT

The emirates are situated in the earth's dry zone, on the edge of the Rub al-Khali Desert. Great technical efforts are being made to prevent the desert from spreading further, as water – in contrast to oil – is a scarce commodity in this region. Millions of shrubs, trees and flowers are artificially irrigated in Dubai. In spite of the meagre resources of ground water, which is brought to the surface from deep boreholes, Dubai's water consumption is among the highest in the world. On a list compiled by the World Wide Fund for Nature (WWF),

Dubai is still one of the biggest wasters of water. The emirate will have to be more careful in its use of this resource, but this will probably only happen gradually. Water is more scarce than crude oil in Dubai, and a bottle of it sometimes costs more than a litre of petrol. Water is supplied from seawater desalination plants, which are energy-intensive and are operated using a great deal of oil or natural gas, and pumped into the city or through long pipelines to golf courses and settlements in the desert.

A companion in the desert: the camel

# THE PERFECT DAY
## Dubai in 24 hours

### 09:00am AN ORIENTAL START THE DAY

Start the day with caffè latte and muesli or mint tea and pita bread beneath the sandalwood tree in the courtyard of the Arabian-style *Basta Arts Café* → p. 50 (photo left). Oriental decor, a colourful mix of customers and a small section selling crafts create a great atmosphere in this café-restaurant.

### 10:00am AROUND OLD DUBAI

After that take a stroll through *Bastakiya* → p. 28, the district that shows the historic roots of Dubai. Old, carefully restored merchants' residences and wind-tower houses in soft desert colours are now home to galleries, boutiques and restaurants, and a guesthouse.

### 11:00am TIME-TRAVEL IN THE MUSEUM

Dubai's wonderful old fort is also in Bastakiya. Its newly built underground wing houses the superb *Dubai Museum* → p. 30 (photo centre). Exhibitions about life in the desert, a reconstruction of an old lane of craft workshops and a Koran school – there is lots to explore.

### 00:30pm BREAK ON THE CREEK

Along souk roads you can walk to the Creek, where the smells of diesel oil and the sea mingle. Workers from India and Pakistan come to sit by the banks, and you can find a seat yourself on the terrace of the old trading house *Bayt al-Wakeel* → p. 57, order a glass of freshly pressed mango juice and watch what's going on the Creek.

### 01:30pm ACROSS THE WATER

With a wooden *water taxi, called an abra* → p. 33, you can join a dozen other passengers from all over the world to cross to the other side. Make sure you have some small change handy, as the crossing costs only one dirham.

### 01:45pm SOUKS AND LUNCH WITH A VIEW

On this side of Dubai, Deira, you can stroll through the streets of souks and bustling commercial quarters to the gold, spice and textile souks, then on to the

# Discover Dubai at its best: in the thick of things, relaxed – and all in a single day

Twin Towers on the Creek. When you get there, take the lift to the *Apple Restaurant (self-service)* → p. 57, and head straight for the outdoor terrace on the third floor for a view of the Creek.

### `04:00pm` OVER TO THE ISLAND

From the Twin Towers it's best to take a taxi through the Shindagha Tunnel to the Gateway Station of the Palm Jumeirah. From here the *monorail* → p. 44 takes you across to the artificial palm-shaped island. From the elevated monorail you get a fantastic view of the sea, yachts and villas, to arrive at the spectacular *Hotel Atlantis* → p. 45, where you can admire the aquariums.

### `05:30pm` LEISURELY STROLL

Back at the Gateway Station, order a taxi to take you along Al Sufouh Road to *Madinat Jumeirah* → p. 44. This superb hotel complex has modern shops in the old Arabian style, trendy cafés and a view of the watery world of the man-made lagoon system of Madinat Jumeirah.

### `07:30pm` PROSECCO AND VEGETARIAN DELIGHTS

One of the many *abras* that are reserved for hotel guests and diners at the restaurant will transport you from the souk to the high-class vegetarian restaurant *Magnolia* → p. 54. Here you can enjoy a wholesome and delicious meal, washed down with a glass of ice-old prosecco. If you are travelling on a budget, eat at one of the many fashionable self-service restaurants in Madinat Jumeirah.

### `10:00pm` NIGHTCAP

Take a taxi to the *Buddha Bar* → p. 68 (ground floor of the Grosvenor Hotel), one of the coolest entertainment spots in town. It's hip, luxurious and expensive. Before you indulge in a cocktail here, why not take an evening walk on the *Dubai Marina* → p. 42 (photo right).

**Metro to the start: Green Line Station: Saeediya**

# SIGHTSEEING

**CITY** **WHERE TO START?**

If you want to see **Old Dubai**, the best place to start is the **Saeediya** Metro station (Green Line). From here head for the restored historic Bastakiya quarter. Then it's not far to the banks of the Creek, at the heart of the original settlement, and the Dubai Museum in the old Al Fahidi fort. Explore modern **Downtown Dubai** – including the world's tallest building, the Burj Khalifa, the colossal Dubai Mall and the man-made Dubai Lake – from the **Dubai Mall** station (Red Line).

The scene hasn't changed in more than a century: fat-bellied dhows, heavily laden and just in from Iran or Yemen, are unloaded on the banks of the Creek. On the quayside wooden crates are piled up. Aden, Mumbai, Karachi and Zanzibar – the next destinations are chalked up on boards.

Today as in bygone times, the *Dubai Creek,* Al-Khor, an inlet of the sea stretching seven miles inland, is the city's vital artery and the foundation of its wealth as a trading port. To the south of the Creek lies the district of Bur Dubai with the historic *Bastakiya* quarter and the oldest merchants' houses in the emirate. Here, as in Deira, the district on the north bank of the Creek, Dubai is noisy, lively and oriental, crammed full with goods

Boomtown in the desert –
Dubai is the city of superlatives:
hyper-modern, luxurious, exciting

from the Far East. You will find old souks, cheap Indian restaurants, low-cost hotels and lots of sights to see. Further south the *World Trade Centre* marks the start of the miles-long *Sheikh Zayed Road,* where the skyscrapers with the most striking architecture line up one beside the other; here stands the gigantic *Burj Khalifa,* the world's tallest building, and the district of *Downtown Dubai* that was built with it. Parallel to Sheikh Zayed Road, *Jumeirah Road* (formerly Jumeirah Beach Road) runs along the sea shore. This is the pre-mier address of Dubai's luxurious beach hotels. As you fly in, before landing there is a good view of the man-made islands in the shape of palms.

# BUR DUBAI

**The history of the emirate began in the 18th century in Bur Dubai ('Dubai-side') at the southwestern end of the Creek.**
The historic wind tower houses in *Basta-kiya* are still crowded together in narrow

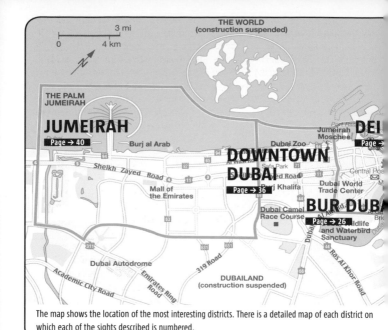

The map shows the location of the most interesting districts. There is a detailed map of each district on which each of the sights described is numbered.

lanes. Hardly any Dubai locals live here now: the houses have been restored at great cost and now accommodate offices, cafés and shops. The centre of Bur Dubai around the old fort is lively and multicultural. People from Afghanistan and India, Sri Lanka and the Philippines live and work here. Indian cut-price stores, cheap Pakistani restaurants, and the colours, sounds and smells of every part of Asia accompany a stroll around the district. Pay a visit to the Dubai Museum and then take a break in one of the Arabian cafés. You can get around well on foot here!

### ■1 BASTAKIYA ★ ● (U C3) (*𝄞 V4*)

In Bastakiya one period in the development of historic Dubai comes to life: the 50 or so houses of the old quarter

were built of mud-brick and coral stone by Persian merchants in the early 20th century. Their characteristic feature is the addition of wind towers that rise above the low houses and by means of an ingenious method of construction channel cooling winds into the interiors – air-conditioning without fossil fuels. In the **INSIDER TIP** publicly accessible buildings such as the *XVA Gallery,* the *Orient Guest House,* the *Bastakiya Nights* restaurant and the *Al-Ahmadiya School* museum (in Deira) you can look at wind towers up close. In recent years an awareness of the cultural importance of the decaying houses evolved, and the quarter was almost entirely restored. Today these historic buildings lie in a traffic-free zone and house restaurants, cafés and two hotels in the traditional Arabian style *(Ori-*

*ent Guest House and XVA Gallery; see p. 80).* Bastakiya is also the site of several of Dubai's galleries. Guided tours can be booked at the *Sheikh Mohammed Centre for Cultural Understanding (Sun–Thu 9am–3pm | 50 Dh | Historic Building | Al-Seef Road | Bastakiya | tel. 3 53 66 66 | www.cultures.ae). Metro Green Line: Saeediya*

### 2 INSIDER TIP BAYT AL-WAKEEL ☀ (U B2) (𝕞 V4)

Drink in the atmosphere on the wooden café terrace of this traditional commercial building ('House of the Agent') of 1934 with its two-storey arcades directly above the Creek: the ceaseless coming and going of abra passengers, the boat traffic on the Creek and the view of the high-rises in Deira. *Bur Dubai Souk, between the two abra stops | Metro Green Line: Al-Ghubaiba*

### 3 BUR DUBAI SOUK (U B–C2) (𝕞 V4)

To enter the long, covered souk lane, you pass through two old wooden gates. Business was flourishing here well over a century ago. The shops, newly built in historic style, exude a mood of nostalgia, which turns into a commercial bustle in the evening. The items on sale here are silks, brocades and pashmina cloths from India and China, with a huge assortment and lots of room for bargaining. *Between the abra stops | Metro Green Line: Al-Ghubaiba*

### 4 CREEKSIDE PARK (110 C5) (𝕞 V6)

Ideal for a leisurely stroll along the Creek: the paths in this 1.5-mile-long park are bordered by flowers and tropical plants, and illuminated in the evenings. The highlight is a ☀ INSIDER TIP cabin lift that passes overhead at a height of 25 m, offering a wonderful view of the Creek and the city skyline. Restaurants and performances at an open-air theatre attract plenty of visitors. *Daily 8am–11pm | between Garhoud Bridge and Maktoum Bridge | Umm Hurair | admission 5 Dh, cable lift 25 Dh | Metro: Healthcare City, Green Line*

---

⭐ **Bastakiya**
The roots of the city lie between the fort and the Creek → p. 28

⭐ **Dubai Museum**
A historic fort is home to the city's largest and most interesting museum → p. 30

⭐ **Sheikh Saeed Al-Maktoum House**
A visit to the old palace of the ruling family → p. 31

⭐ **Dubai Marina**
Marina and skyscrapers → p. 42

⭐ **Burj Khalifa**
The world's tallest building → p. 37

⭐ **Trip on the Creek**
A mini-cruise on the Creek: a cheap and enjoyable trip on a dhow → p. 33

⭐ **Al-Khor Corniche**
Heavily laden dhows put in on Dubai Creek for unloading → p. 35

⭐ **Burj Al Arab**
The emblem of Dubai – and also the world's most luxurious and famous hotel → p. 41

⭐ **Hotel Atlantis**
'Only' a hotel on the man-made island of Palm Jumeirah, but a sight in its own right → p. 45

**MARCO POLO HIGHLIGHTS**

## ⑤ DUBAI MUSEUM ★ (U C3) (📖 V4)

The long, brightly limewashed rooms are used to exhibit crafts, ancient-looking rifles, tools associated with the pearl fishery and traditional boats. The ● lower

Testimony to the past:
a well in the Dubai Museum

floor is dedicated to everyday life in Dubai before the oil boom. Visitors walk along the lanes of a souk as it was in Dubai 50 years ago. Life-size figures represent craftsmen and merchants at their work, accompanied by the appropriate background noises. The depictions of the life of desert animals by day and by night and of life in an oasis are also inter-

esting. The home of the museum is the *Al-Fahidi Fort,* which was built 200 years ago – which makes it one of the oldest structures in Dubai. *Sat–Thu 8.30am–8pm, Fri 2.30–8.30pm| Al-Fahidi Fort Al-Fahidi Street | admission 3 Dh | Metro: Saeediya, Green Line*

## ⑥ DUBAI MUNICIPALITY MUSEUM (U C2) (📖 V4)

This museum on the Creek (near the abra quay) and at the entrance to the Spice Souk is small but well worth seeing. It occupies a two-storey house in the old Arabian style with wooden balconies all round, and was the seat of the city administration from 1957 until 1964. The rooms, traditionally furnished in plain Arabian style, are given over to a photographic documentation of the rise of Dubai. *Sat–Thu 8am–3pm | Baniyas Road | free admission | Metro Green Line: Saeediya*

## ⑦ GRAND MOSQUE (U C3) (📖 V4)

The Grand Mosque was built in 1996–98 between the Al-Fahidi Fort and the Creek. A 70 m (230 ft) minaret, the city's tallest, towers above the principal mosque of Bur Dubai, which has nine large and 45 smaller domes, as well as sand-coloured walls, wooden window grilles and leaded-light windows. *Not open to visitors | Al-Fahidi R/A, near the Ruler's Court | Metro Green Line: Saeediya*

## ⑧ HERITAGE & DIVING VILLAGE ● (U C1) (📖 V4)

Next to the Sheikh Saeed al-Maktoum House find a monument to the Bedouin heritage of the emirate, the period before the oil boom and pearl fishing: reconstructions of mud-brick buildings with wind towers grouped around large expanses of sand. They house photographic exhibitions and shops selling crafts, col-

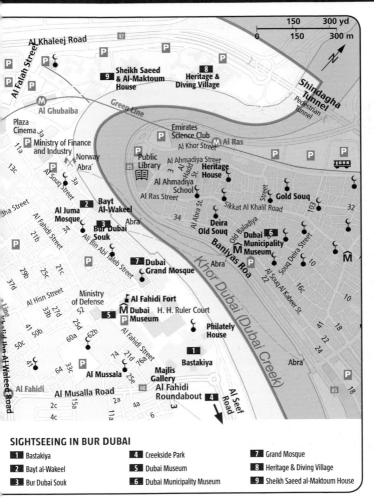

## SIGHTSEEING IN BUR DUBAI

**1** Bastakiya
**2** Bayt al-Wakeel
**3** Bur Dubai Souk
**4** Creekside Park
**5** Dubai Museum
**6** Dubai Municipality Museum
**7** Grand Mosque
**8** Heritage & Diving Village
**9** Sheikh Saeed al-Maktoum House

ourful shells and culinary specialities.
The *Diving Village* next door is entered through an antique wooden gate decorated with nautical motifs. The prize exhibits are a large number of varied ships' models. The implements that male pearl-divers used are also on display. Directly adjacent to the Heritage & Diving Village there are several fish restaurants, where diners sit outdoors right by the Creek. *Sat–Thu 8.30am–10pm, Fri 3–10pm | Shindagha Road, Bur Dubai side of the mouth of the Creek | free admission | Metro Green Line: Al Ghubaiba*

**9** **SHEIKH SAEED AL-MAKTOUM HOUSE** ★ (U C1) (*∅ V4*)

Shindagha, the historic quarter on the Creek, is the site of the magnificent palace of Sheikh Saeed al-Maktoum (1912–

58), the grandfather of the present emir, who is regarded as the founder of modern Dubai. Saeed and the six families of his clan lived in this two-storey building, whose 30 rooms are still cooled by the characteristic wind towers. Exactly 100 years after it was built, in 1996, the palace, much of it reconstructed, was opened to the public as a museum. It contains various exhibitions, including about traditional life in the desert. *Sat–Thu 8.30am–8pm, Fri 3–9.30pm | Shindagha Road, next to the Heritage & Diving Village | admission 2 Dh | Metro Green Line: Al Ghubaiba*

# DEIRA

**The souks of Deira give you a first impression of the importance of Dubai as a historic trading port and the mentality of its people.**

Spices and gold, electronics and clothing – shops line the lanes and streets of the quarter, where bargaining goes on round the clock with the exception of the times of prayer. Back in the 19th century local and Iranian families of traders set up in Deira on the north side of the Creek and founded the largest souk on the whole Gulf coast here at the tip of land by the Creek known as *Al-Ras*. Modern high-rises with striking design put their stamp on the Baniyas waterfront road, where dozens of traditional wooden dhows are moored. In Deira the merchants' Dubai is still alive and all kinds of goods are offered for sale until late in the evening, and the Indian and Pakistani restaurants also stay open late.

Classic Arabian air-conditioning: wind tower in the Heritage Village

### ■ INSIDER TIP AL-AHMADIYA SCHOOL
● (U C2) (*Ⱳ V4*)

Arcades, courtyards and a 7 m-high wind tower: Dubai's first school, dating from 1912, has had a thorough restoration. Lettering in relief with verses from the Koran decorates the high-ceilinged rooms. The school was originally intended for adult men, and another 20 years passed before the sons of the ruling family and of rich merchants were educated here. *Sat–Thu 8am–7.30pm, Fri 2.30–7.30pm | 19 Street (from Al-Ras Street) | free admission | Metro Green Line: Al Ras*

### ■ CROSSING THE CREEK ↯↯
(U B–C2, U D3) (*Ⱳ V4*)

The ultra-modern skyscraper architecture of the Deira waterfront and the historic, honey-coloured buildings of the Bastakiya quarter are divided by the city's lifeline, the sluggishly flowing Creek. It can be crossed using the Shindagha Tunnel and four bridges. But the best way to get across is a ⭐ *trip over the Creek* with one of the open wooden boats known as *abras*, which can take about 20 passengers. The boats, which are often moored four-deep, make the crossing round the clock as soon as enough passengers have arrived, which usually takes only a few minutes. This enjoyable trip costs one dirham (1 Dh). During the ten-minute crossing you have a panoramic view of the city skyline and the traditional Bastakiya quarter. The boats depart in Deira and opposite on the Bur-Dubai bank from two abra docks each side.

### 3 INSIDER TIP ▶ DEIRA FISH MARKET
(U E1–2) (*W4*)

Baskets, crates, shells, heaps, buckets full of fish: on tables and on the floor of these market halls, with everything from sardines to sharks, not forgetting crabs, shrimps, langoustines and lobsters, and blue-clad workers who clean and cut up the fish. *Daily 7am–noon and 7–10pm | Al-Khaleej Road (Deira Corniche, next to the Hyatt Regency) | Metro Green Line: Palm Deira*

### 4 DUBAI CREEK GOLF & YACHT CLUB
(110 C5) (*V6*)

This course, created in 1993 by American golf-course designer Karl Litten, delights non-golfers too thanks to its exceptionally beautiful landscaping and the memorable design of the clubhouse. Looking like an Arab dhow with its enormous sails, this is one of the outstanding emblems of the new Dubai. In the clubhouse of the marina, which lies directly on the Creek and looks like a hyper-modern ocean liner, there are several 🍴 restaurants and cafés providing their guests

Lovingly restored and opened as a museum in 1997: the Al-Ahmadiya School

with some of the best views of the Dubai skyline. *The Boardwalk (daily 8am–1am | Moderate)* with terraces above the Creek serves international food, *Aquarium (daily midday–3pm and 7–11pm | Expensive)* specialises in fish dishes, *Lake-view (daily 6.30am–10.30pm | Moderate)* has a casual international style. *Al-Garhoud, opposite Deira City Centre | green fee 595–795 Dh | tel. 2 95 60 00 (also for the restaurants) | www.dubaigolf.com | Metro Red Line: Deira City Centre*

## 5 GOLD SOUK (U D2) (*Ⅲ V4*)

Asian, European and Russian visitors all come here – the Gold Souk with more than 300 stores where gold jewellery is sold almost exclusively by weight is not only a place for shopping but also one of the sights of the city. Dubai is known around the world as an important centre of the gold trade, and the sign reading 'City of Gold' at the entrance to the souk truly is a fitting description of the city. You can still sense the authentic atmosphere of a souk where bargaining has been going on for decades. *Daily 9.30am–1pm and 4–10pm | Sikkat al-Khail Street | Metro Green Line: Al Ras*

## 6 INSIDER TIP HERITAGE HOUSE (U C2) (*Ⅲ V4*)

This museum lets you look behind the scenes of middle-class life in Dubai in the early 20th century. This house, built in 1890 in the traditional Arabian style, was extended to a size of over 900 m$^2$ in 1910 by the owner of the day. From the courtyard you have access to a *majlis,* a reception and assembly room for men, adorned with verses from the Koran and weapons. The sparsely furnished rooms, the modest number of personal possessions, most of them functional, hand-made and of a high aesthetic standard, makes an impression of timeless beauty and provides a relaxing experience. *Sat–*

Strikingly beautiful: the elegant clubhouse in the Dubai Creek Golf & Yacht Club

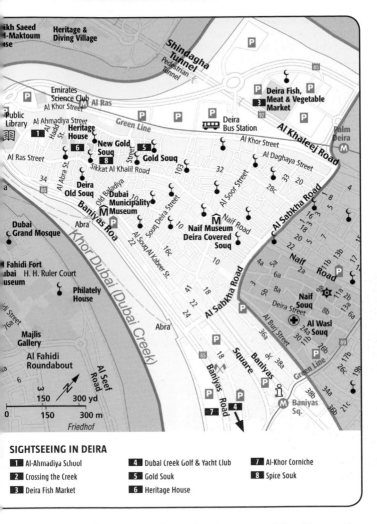

## SIGHTSEEING IN DEIRA

**1** Al-Ahmadiya School
**2** Crossing the Creek
**3** Deira Fish Market
**4** Dubai Creek Golf & Yacht Club
**5** Gold Souk
**6** Heritage House
**7** Al-Khor Corniche
**8** Spice Souk

*Thu 8am–7.30pm, Fri 2.30–7.30pm | 19 Street, opposite 14 Sikka (next to the Al-Ahmadiya School) | free admission | Metro Green Line: Al-Ras*

## **7** AL-KHOR CORNICHE ★
(U C2–D6) (*∭ V4*)

The smell of the salty sea mingles with oriental aromas and diesel fumes: Al-Khor Corniche, *Baniyas Road* on the banks of the Creek, presents a refreshing contrast to the glamour and materialism that mark Dubai today. For decades fat-bellied, heavily laden dhows have anchored three and four deep by the quay walls of the Dubai Creek. Boxes

Smell, taste and listen to the traders: the Spice Souk is a feast for the senses

and sacks, mattresses and bolts of fabric, car tyres and much, much more is unloaded from the ships and stored on the waterfront. *Baniyas Road, between Al-Maktoum Bridge and Al-Ras | Metro Green Line: Baniyas Square*

### 8 SPICE SOUK (U D2) (𝄞 V4)

In the narrow lanes of the Spice Souk little shops are crowded together. There is a delicious smell of cardamom, cloves and coriander, traders from Pakistan sell cinnamon sticks, peppercorns and henna from jute sacks. Coffee and tea, nuts, almonds and pistachios, saffron and dried fruit are also on offer. *Sat–Thu 8am–1pm and 4–10pm, Fri 4–10pm | Al-Ras Street (next to the Gold Souk) | Metro Green Line: Al Ras*

# DOWNTOWN DUBAI

**Sheikh Zayed Road, Dubai's 'palace boulevard', is more than just a traffic artery. The heart of the new Dubai beats along this road.**

Stretching for miles on up to twelve lanes, *Sheikh Zayed Road* runs south parallel to *Jumeirah Road*. Some sixty skyscrapers with this prestigious address have so far been built. The thoroughfare starts in the north at Dubai's *World Trade Centre*, constructed in 1979 as the city's first high-rise office block, and far from the centre at the time. In recent years Sheikh Zayed Road has grown at breathtaking speed from a two-lane country road to an emblem of the new city. A letterhead bearing the name of the road is a must for every large or ambitious company in Dubai, and to live here is a status symbol for business people and a pleasure for the rich. Near Sheikh Zayed Road the *Burj Khalifa*, Dubai's tallest building, rises to the heavens. For a fine spectacle here go to the ● *Dubai Fountain* in the Dubai Lake, a superb combination of water, lights and sound.

Downtown Dubai is the name of the new city district at the foot of this skyscraper. Here you will find not only several top attractions (next to the Burj Khalifa is the Dubai Mall), but also an atmospheric place to take a stroll along the man-made Dubai Lake. Glamour and commerce meet in the cafés and shops of this district in a skilful copy of oriental styles. Superb wood-carvings and narrow, dimly lit lanes of shops are the characteristic feature of the Souk Al-Bahar, but only a few paces away lies a gigantic temple to the consumer world, the Dubai Mall. This mix of the hyper-modern and copies of the ancient orient may be somewhat confusing to people new to the city, but it is typical of Downtown Dubai. Everything that the people of the emirate love is united here: tradition and modern superlatives. Sheikh Zayed Road and in Downtown Dubai boasts hotels, restaurants, clubs, shops and shopping malls for a well-to-do elite of western expatriates, who are on the go here until after midnight.

■ **1** **BURJ KHALIFA** ★ ● (U E9) (*M S5*)
Dubai currently holds the gold medal in the tower-building Olympics: its landmark reaches over 2600 ft into the sky, tapering at the top. With its silver-gleaming aluminium façade, 163 storeys and 57 lifts, this tower *(burj)* is the world's tallest building. It houses offices, apartments, restaurants and clubs, pools, gyms and a hotel: floors 5 to 8 and 38 to 39 are occupied by Giorgio Armani's design hotel. The Burj Khalifa has a ☼ viewing deck on the 124th (!) floor at a height of 1450 ft. Tickets are sold in the Dubai Mall at the 'At the Top' ticket desk. From there a moving walkway takes you across to the Burj

# BOOKS & FILMS

▶ **Father of Dubai** – A life of Sheikh Rashid bin Saeed Al-Maktoum (by Graeme Wilson, 1999).

▶ **Dubai Tales** – These short stories by Muhammad al Murr provide an insight into life in the emirate. The author's Wink of the Mona Lisa is also well worth reading.

▶ **Arabian Sands** – Wilfred Thesiger's classic travel book describes his journeys in the age before oil was discovered.

▶ **Syriana** – A political thriller about oil made in 2005 (director: Stephen Gaghan) starring George Clooney and Matt Damon. The desert landscape of Dubai and the UAE provided the backdrop for the action.

▶ **Dubai Dubai** – DVD released in 2010 that offers a good introduction to the emirate.

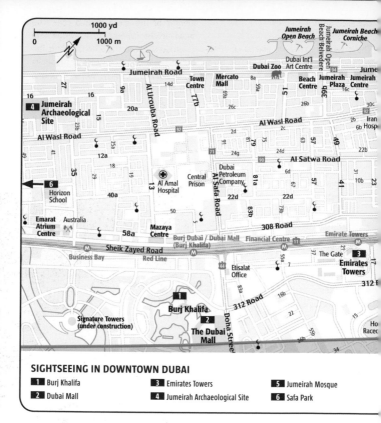

## SIGHTSEEING IN DOWNTOWN DUBAI

**1** Burj Khalifa
**2** Dubai Mall
**3** Emirates Towers
**4** Jumeirah Archaeological Site
**5** Jumeirah Mosque
**6** Safa Park

Khalifa, past a large model of the building, to a two-storey lift that conveys visitors to the viewing deck in one minute without stopping. Tickets to visit straight away cost 400 Dh, whereas the price for reserving a later visit is 100 Dh (children up to 12 years 75 Dh). *Sun–Wed 10am–10pm, Thu–Sat 10am–midnight. Sheikh Zayed Road, 1st Interchange (Doha Street) | www.burjkhalifa.ae | Metro Red Line: Dubai Mall*

**2** **DUBAI MALL** (109 D4) *(ψ S5)* ●
This shopping mall and leisure complex contains approx. 1200 shops, the *Dubai Aquarium & Underwater Zoo (see p. 88)*, the Olympic-standard *Dubai Ice Rink (see p. 88)*, a gold souk, an enormous multiplex cinema, and 160 cafés and restaurants. INSIDER TIP The Dubai Mall operates twelve shuttle bus routes from all parts of the city to the mall free of charge. They run between various hotels and the bus stop in the Dubai Mall, where timetables are available, and are also a good way of getting a free tour of the city. *Daily 10am–midnight | Doha Street (from Sheikh Zayed Road), 1st Interchange | www.thedubaimall.com | Metro Red Line: Dubai Mall*

### 3 EMIRATES TOWERS
(109 E3) (*m T5*)

These two skyscrapers, placed close together with their triangular ground plan and a height of over 980 ft, are visible from far away. The *Emirates Office Tower* is houses mainly offices, while the *Jumeirah Emirates Hotel Tower* is home to the luxury hotel belonging to the group of that name. At ground level the two towers are connected by the *Emirates Towers Shopping Boulevard. Sheikh Zayed Road | www.jumeirahemiratestowers.com | Metro Red Line: Emirates Towers*

### 4 JUMEIRAH ARCHAEOLOGICAL SITE
(108 B2) (*m R4*)

After many years of effort on the part of the Jordanian head archaeologist, the most significant excavation site in Dubai was opened to the public in 2005. The finds relate to a settlement over 1000 years old on a strategic site between Mesopotamia and Oman, which were trading partners. The 20-acre site lay by the sea at that time. In the 18th century the site was built over, and only foundations about one metre high remain of the original buildings: several residences with courtyards, workshops and shops, a mosque, a caravanserai and a market. *Sun–Thu 9am–1pm, visits at present available only through travel agents | Jumeirah I, between Al-Wasl Road and Jumeirah Road (from 27 Street), entrance at the corner of 16 Street/33 Street | Metro Red Line: Business Bay*

### 5 JUMEIRAH MOSQUE
(U E9) (*m T4*)

The city's largest mosque, and in the opinion of many its most beautiful when seen from outside, is a domed building that was built from ivory-coloured limestone in 1983. It is flanked by two minarets, and columns bear the weight of the great domed roof. The prayer niche *(mihrab)* is as everywhere oriented to Mecca, and to its right is the pulpit *(mimbar)*. The doors of mosques in the emirate normally remain closed to non-believers, but the Jumeirah Mosque is an exception. The *Sheikh Mohammed Centre for Cultural Understanding (see p. 25)* offers hour-long INSIDER TIP guided tours of the mosque *(meeting point*

Dubai's skyline with the twin Emirates Towers

Sat, Sun, Tue, Thu in front of the mosque, opposite The One furniture store | registration (10 Dh) from 9am, tour 10–11.15 am). Men may not wear shorts, women will be given a black robe (abaya) and a headscarf. *Jumeirah Road | www.cultures. ae | Metro Red Line: Trade Centre*

### ■6 SAFA PARK (108 B2–3) (*Ⅲ Q4–5*)

This 160-acre landscaped park is one of the oldest and loveliest parks in Dubai. As long ago as 1975 it was created between Sheikh Zayed Road and Al-Wasl Road for the residents of the Jumeirah

The Jumeirah Mosque opens its doors to non-believers

district. Today it contains almost 20,000 trees and shrubs of many different kinds, some of them in the so-called model gardens, which are based on oriental and European gardens. There are also jogging circuits here. *Daily 8am–midnight | Al-Safa | admission 3 Dh | Metro Red Line: Business Bay*

# JUMEIRAH

**This is where Dubai makes dreams of sunny beach holidays come true. Several luxurious and beautiful hotels adorn the miles of ● Jumeirah Beach, and the world-famous Burj Al Arab spreads its sails here.**

If you drive south on the long *Jumeirah Road* (formerly *Jumeirah Beach Road*), the sea is on your right. In between, concealed in dense greenery and behind palm trees, lie the fine residences of wealthy locals and the palaces of the ruling family. Jumeirah is not only the place of choice to live but also the leisure and pleasure strip for Arabian society: quays for yachts, parks, resorts and hotels whose architecture, furnishings and room prices aim to break records line up here one next to the other. And the view offshore shows how Dubai is carrying through its huge projects: *The Palm Jumeirah* and *The World,* artificial islands that fulfil any dream you want by creating a Caribbean or South Seas feeling in an Arabian city. In Jumeirah no-one gets around on foot: you take a taxi or a tour coach. Luxury limousines queue in front of the Royal Mirage Hotel. Dubai residents in white dishdashas stroll to the entrance accompanied by their elegant and extremely beautiful wives: the hotels of Jumeirah Beach are home to rich Emiratis, who are rarely spotted in their home country but can be seen here if anywhere.

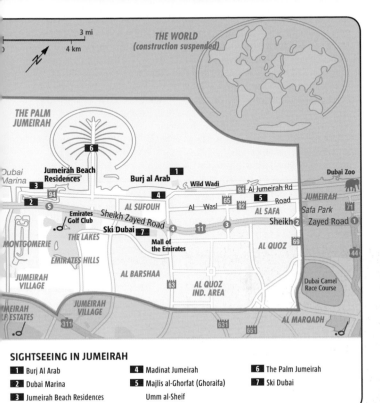

### **1** BURJ AL ARAB ★ (U D9) (*M N3*)

Raspberry red morphs into grass green and pale turquoise: after dark the Teflon sail of the Burj Al Arab shimmers like a tropical bird and changes colour every 15 minutes. When it opened in 1999 this hotel brought worldwide publicity to Dubai and marked its rise to a top-class holiday destination. The 'Arabian Tower', which cost around 1.2 billion US dollars, was placed in the sea on a man-made island 300 m (985 ft) from the beach. It is 1053 ft tall and accommodates 202 suites, all between 169 and 780 m² in size. At the time of completion it was the emblem of the emirate, designed as a stylised dhow sail filled by the wind. The circular platform on the 28th floor is a helicopter landing pad. Next to the escalators leading from the ground floor into the hotel foyer, jets of water spurt 30 m (100 ft) high from the floor, a light show in all the colours of the rainbow providing a dazzling accompaniment to the fountain. If you want to enter, you need a reservation in one of the restaurants, cafés or bars. For lunch, perhaps, in *Al-Mahara* (a restaurant with underwater atmosphere, see p. 52) or in 🌿 *Al-Muntaha,* the 'Heavenly View' restaurant at a height of 656 m (2150 ft) with a fantastic view of Dubai and the beach. You make a booking by credit card and receive a reservation number to show at the entrance. Or you can book a city tour including a visit to Burj Al Arab or even a special Burj Al Arab tour at a travel agent. Further alternatives are tea-time and Friday brunch, booked on the hotel website with a reservation code to allow you admission to the building. Depending on the restaurant and the time of day, expect the adventure to set you back some 250–600 Dh per person. *Jumeirah Road | tel. 04 3 01 76 00 and 04 3 01 77 77 | www.burj-al-arab.com | Metro Red Line: First Gulf Bank*

### ■2 DUBAI MARINA ★ ●
(104 B–C1) (*Ⓜ J4*)

A land-locked marina: an artificial channel 2.5 miles long creates a maritime atmosphere and a change of scenery. And, typically for Dubai, 200 high-rises with striking architecture, several of them topping 300 m, are going up around it. The star of the scene here will be the *Pentominium.* When it is finished, its height of 516 m (1692 ft) will make it the world's tallest residential building, and it will be one of the most luxurious and expensive

# BEACHES

There is an *open beach* south of Dubai Marine Beach Resort *(Jumeirah Road, Jumeirah 1)*. A beach park that can be recommended is the 30-acre ● *Jumeirah Beach Park (Sun–Wed 8am–10pm, Thu–Sat until 11pm | Mon only women and children | Jumeirah Road, Jumeirah 2 | admission 5 Dh)* with a sandy beach 700 m (2300 ft) long, palms, well-kept lawns and loungers, a self-service kiosk and facilities for playing volleyball. Lots of tourists and expats come to relax here. The green *Al-Mamzar Beach Park*, which features tall date palms, exotic trees, flowers and extensive lawns, is situated at the northwestern edge of the city on the border to Sharjah. It boasts five sandy beaches no less, on the sea and around a lagoon with shallow water, as well as three pools, bike hire, changing rooms, showers and restaurants. Although the park covers an area of 250 acres, its gets full on Fridays and Saturdays. *Daily 8am–10.30pm | Wed is family day: men cannot come on their own | Hamriya | admission 5 Dh or 30 Dh per car incl. driver and passengers, pool 10 Dh*

Skyscrapers are essential in this city, even for mooring yachts: the Dubai Marina

to boot *(www.pentominium.com)*.

Here you can take a tour of the city by boat, as *dhow cruises* are on offer at the Dubai Marina. The one-hour daytime trip passes through the marina and past the den Jumeirah Beach Residences, the Palm Jumeirah with its Atlantis Hotel and the Burj Al Arab *(4 x daily, 60 Dh, www. dubaimarinacruise.com)*. The two-hour *dinner cruise (8.30pm, 195 Dh)* also starts out from the Dubai Marina Promenade West.

From October to April the INSIDER TIP *Marina Market*, where crafts and souvenirs are on sale, takes place every Friday and Saturday on *Marina Walk* (opposite Grosvenor House). *The Dubai Marina is situated – with a direct connection to Sheikh Zayed Road – approx. 16 mi southwest of the city centre at Interchange 5 | Metro Red Line: Dubai Marina*

### ■3 JUMEIRAH BEACH RESIDENCES
(104 B1) (∅ J3)

The highlight of this district is *The Walk*,

a mile-long shopping boulevard that has brought a Mediterranean, urban atmosphere to the waterfront thanks to arcades, fountains and jets of water shooting high into the air. Although it is still all a bit artificial, the only outdoor shopping street on the sea quickly gained its clientele. About 200 boutiques are housed in buildings with a classical design and new luxurious residential towers as a backdrop. It is planned that the Jumeirah Beach Residences quarter will have a population of 25,000 one day. *Between The Palm Jumeirah and Dubai Marina | www.jumeirahbeachresidences.com | Metro Red Line: Jumeirah Lake Towers*

### ■4 MADINAT JUMEIRAH
(106 B1) (∅ M4)

Seen from the air, it looks like an Arabian village: enormous multi-storey buildings in the traditional Arabian style and the colour of brown clay, with added wind towers, delicate wooden balcony grilles, arcades and terraces, bordered by broad watercourses on which electrically powered *abras* glide to and fro.

Madinat Jumeirah (Jumeirah City) is just an illusion, however, as nothing here is old and weathered, and two hotels have been inserted into these artificially created surroundings. Nevertheless, these gigantic Arabian palaces are well worth seeing and provide a contrast to the rest of the skyscraper architecture. There is also a replica of a traditional souk, but it is a sterile place and hardly worth visiting considering the many genuine souks that can be seen in Dubai. The adjacent restaurants and cafés are a much more attractive proposition. *Jumeirah Road | www.madinatjumeirah.com | Metro Red Line: Mall of the Emirates*

### ▪5 MAJLIS AL-GHORFAT (GHORAIFA) UMM AL-SHEIF
(108 A2) (*ᗰ Q4*)

A two-storey building made of coral stone, plastered with a roof of palm fronds, was the summer residence of Sheikh Rashid Bin Saeed al-Maktoum, the grandfather of the present emir. It was constructed in 1954 in what was then called Umm Suqueim on the coast south of Dubai, and has been restored at great expense. It is surrounded by a garden and was constructed in the style of the period before the oil boom, then equipped with antique Bedouin carpets, a great many cushions for sitting on and the inevitable display of weapons. The doors and windows have been replaced using teak wood. *Sat–Thu 8.30am–1.30 pm and 2.30–8.30pm, Fri 2–8.30pm | Jumeirah Road south of Jumeirah Beach Park | admission 2 Dh | Metro Red Line: Al-Quoz*

### ▪6 THE PALM JUMEIRAH
(U C8) (*ᗰ K–L 2–3*)

The man-made island opposite Jumei-

rah Beach has the shape of a palm tree and consists of a 'trunk' just over a mile long and 17 'palm fronds' in addition to a breakwater surrounding the island that is known as *The Crescent.* The fronds house villas costing millions, some of them set very close together as if they were estates of terraced houses. Along the trunk there is a marina with 600 moorings for yachts. Beyond the fronds and just before it reaches The Crescent, the road descends into a tunnel and emerges into daylight again at the luxurious Hotel Atlantis. *The Palm Jumeirah | Al-Sufouh Road | www.thepalm.ae | Metro Red Line: Nakheel*

A INSIDER TIP monorail runs from the Gateway Station on the coast by the Royal Mirage Hotel across The Palm Jumeirah to the Hotel Atlantis, stopping twice on the way *(15 Dh, return 25 Dh).*

★ *Hotel Atlantis* (1539 rooms) on the Crescent is an opulent pink palace with towers and turrets. The interior of the Hotel Atlantis is a crazy sight: columns as high as towers are adorned with reliefs of shells, the door handles have the shape of sea horses and dolphins, pictures of octopuses, corals and sea anemones cover the walls. The *Ambassador Lagoon* aquarium is populated by fluorescent jellyfish, enormous rays and groupers. Those who are not living in the hotel can visit these *Lost Chambers* – so-called because the aquarium is decorated with ruins as a reminder of the legendary lost city of Atlantis – in a system of tunnels. The *Aquaventure* water park *(see p. 80)*, which is open to all visitors, also belongs to the hotel. *The Palm Jumeirah Crescent Road | admission 70 Dh | www.atlantis thepalm.com*

### ■ 7 SKI DUBAI (U D9) (*M5*) ●

6000 tons of snow were used to convert an area the size of three football fields into an indoor skiing arena. At a temperature of minus two Celsius (°F 28), fans of winter sports can enjoy themselves on five downhill slopes. There are tow-lifts and even a proper cabin lift to take visitors back to the top. At a maximum of 400 m (1300 ft) the slopes are not very long, but the level of difficulty varies. 30 tons of artificial snow are added every night, and the meltwater is used to cool the shopping mall. Youngsters of all ages take great delight in the *Snowpark*, where they can slide downhill in plastic tubes. *Daily 10am–11pm | The Mall of the Emirates | Sheikh Zayed Road, 4th Interchange | admission 2 hrs 180 Dh, all day 300 Dh incl. skiing equipment, 120 Dh for the Snowpark | www.skidxb.com | Metro Red Line: Mall of the Emirates*

Winter sports in the desert: at Ski Dubai no expense was spared, except possibly on the decorations

# AROUND DUBAI CITY

**From the air it is plain to see that Dubai is surrounded by desert. Within the city limits, however, this is hardly noticeable at all.**

You don't have to drive far to get the desert feeling. Sand and grey shrubs fringe the multi-lane roads that lead into the desert. The best way to experience this is to take a taxi, which is not expensive and stress-free, to hire a car – e.g. for a drive to the little town of Hatta some 65 miles away – or to book a complete day trip. Note that the route on the highway passes through a few miles of Omani territory, so take your passport to be on the safe side!

## BIG RED (117 D5) (*ω 0*)

The last rays of the sun bathe this 328 ft-high desert dune in the colours of gold and deep red. But instead of a peaceful desert atmosphere there is usually a lot going on here, some 35 miles out of Dubai City (E44): a range of hire companies have quad-bikes, motorbikes with huge, balloon-like tyres on which you can race through the sand and up and down the dunes *(30 minutes for approx. 100 Dh)*. A camel ride is more leisurely, more environmentally sound and cheaper too. Make sure you agree the price before you get on the camel *(about 40 Dh for the half-hour)*.

## HATTA (117 E5) (*ω 0*)

The sleepy little oasis town of Hatta lies among the rugged rocks of the Hatta Mountains. Driving from Dubai on the Hatta Road (E44) you cross fantastic desert landscapes with dunes that glow in a big range of colours depending on the time of day.

The attraction in Hatta is the Heritage Village. A settlement dating back to the 16th century has been rebuilt there using air-dried mud bricks. The old fort too was restored using historic building materials. The ● *Hatta Fort Hotel (tel. 04 8 52 32 11 | www.hattaforthotel. com | 50 rooms | Moderate)* lies in a 75-acre tropical park and has luxurious rooms in the style of a rustic chalet. For dining there is a restaurant and Café Gazebo. At the hotel book a trip out to the *Hatta Pools* in Wadi Qahfi (they are about 10 miles away, and difficult to find unless you know the area): clear water flows all year round in these pool in the granite rocks, and the Emiratis love to come here at weekends for a picnic. *The Hatta Road (E44) starts at the 1st Interchange on Sheikh Zayed Road*. Travel agents and some hotels in Dubai organise the tour to Hatta as a day trip.

# LOW BUDGET

▶ For the cheapest harbour tour, take the *Waterbus (see p. 94)* on its 'tourist route' from Shindagha **(U B1) (*ω V4)*** to Al-Seef Road. *Daily 8am–midnight, hourly | 45 min return trip | 25 Dh | Metro Green Line:* Al Ghubaiba

▶ The view of the city, sea and desert costs 400 Dh from the 124th floor of the Burj Khalifa. For an almost identical view from Bar Neos on the 63rd floor of The Address hotel, which is opposite, you only have to buy a drink *(see p. 76)*. **(U B1) (*ω S5)*** *Metro Red Line: Dubai Mall*

A popular excursion for Emiratis: the Hatta Pools in Oman

## INSIDER TIP MUSEUM OF ISLAMIC CIVILIZATION (116 C3) (𝄞 0)

A golden dome and tall arcades mark this building, which is only a few decades old and was built in a magnificent Islamic style. It is Sharjah's finest museum and one of the best in the United Arab Emirates. The large fascinating collection of Islamic items is presented thematically. 'The five pillars of Islam' on the ground floor provides insights into the Islamic religion and helps non-believers to understand it. Historic black-and-white photos show pilgrims in Mecca, a city that non-Muslims are forbidden to enter. One item is a treasure of unique value for Muslims: a piece of cloth, part of the former covering of the Kaaba in Mecca. This holy relic is displayed behind glass and well protected. *Sun–Thu 8am–8pm | Fri 4–8pm | Al-Majarrah Souk | Al-Majarrah Corniche | Sharjah | admission 5 Dh*

## NAD AL-SHEBA (U E9–10) (𝄞 R8)

Opposite what used to be the track for camel races in Nad Al-Sheba, the

## INSIDER TIP *National Falconry Centre (Muscat Road | Al-Markadh | tel. 04 2 06 34 55)* occupies a wind tower house. Twenty shops in the courtyard sell the equipment used in hunting with falcons, and there are even live birds on sale. It is interesting to watch the dealers and purchasers haggling over prices. There are also exhibitions, a small museum and a café.

In Nad Al-Sheba you can also visit the Meydan Race Course *(see p. 70)*.

## RAS AL-KHOR WILDLIFE & WATERBIRD SANCTUARY (113 F1) (𝄞 T7)

An area of 2.5 sq mi at the inland end of the Creek has been established as a nature reserve to protect and preserve the habitat of migratory birds and some species that permanently live here, including a large colony of flamingos. About 20,000 birds from 90 species have been counted here. There are ☀ three observation towers. *Daily 8am–6pm | Ras al-Khor (5 mi east of Deira) | free admission | Metro Green Line: Creek*

# FOOD & DRINK

**Dubai is quite simply a culinary paradise. Expatriates from all over the world and the region's traditional openness to international gastronomic influences have made their mark on the restaurant scene.**

The city's top gourmet spots and famous upscale restaurants are generally found in the five-star hotels. What goes down particularly well with holidaymakers are the sumptuous buffets for breakfast, lunch and dinner with a combination of international dishes and oriental specialities. Friday brunch is a popular institution in almost all the four- and five-star hotels. Brunch goes on well into the afternoon and is by no means cheap – a price of around 200 Dh is usual; double that amount if you want to wash it down with wine or champagne.

Arabian food in Dubai draws on Lebanese, Egyptian, Yemeni and other influences. The most common meat is traditionally lamb and poultry, less often beef (and pork is generally completely absent). Basmati rice from the slopes of the Himalayas, long-grained with a slightly nutty taste, is frequently used. The most popular vegetables are aubergines, beans, pumpkin, fennel, chard, carrots, cucumber, cauliflower and chickpeas. Vegetable purees are generously seasoned with sesame oil. There is a wide range of fresh fish and crustaceans: the Arabian Gulf and the Indian Ocean yield langoustines, prawns and lobsters, as well as every imaginable kind of fish, including the popular *hammour,* a kind

## Cardamom, coriander & many more exotic delights – the world's cuisines meet in Dubai

of grouper. Spices play a big role in oriental cuisine. It was Arabs who opened up the spice routes to India and China when they started to trade in cardamom, pepper, cinnamon and saffron. The food of the region is still characterised by an unstinting use of spices.

The wide range of restaurants encompasses the gourmet destination restaurants in hotels with fantastic interior design, event gastronomy in desert tents, fast-food outlets in the shopping malls and the restaurants favoured by Asian workers from India and Pakistan, where delicious meals are served at little cost. If you like Indian food, you will dine not only much better but also more cheaply in a small inconspicuous Indian restaurant than at McDonald's and suchlike.

Don't miss out on the national snack *shawarma*, thinly sliced chicken or beef from a rotating grill, stuffed into a pitta bread with salad and tomatoes like a kebab and sold everywhere. There is no need to take great care about eating from street stalls in Dubai, as all the restaurants and

Panoramic teatime in the Skyview Bar of the Burj Al Arab Hotel

snack stalls are run along hygienic lines and meet basic standards. So the good news is that in Dubai you can have a good dinner for 10 Dh or, if you prefer, for 1000 Dh.

Water is drunk with meals. As an aperitif, freshly squeezed fruit juice or a creative fruit cocktail are the order of the day. Only hotel restaurants and a few clubs are licensed to serve alcoholic drinks.

It is hard to find restaurants with genuine cooking from the emirates. The Sheikh Mohammed Centre for Cultural Understanding *(SMCCU, tel. 04 3 53 66 66, www.cultures.ae)* in Bastakiya serves a **INSIDERTIP** *cultural breakfast (Mon, Wed 10am, 50 Dh)* with *lugimat* (balls of dough with date syrup), *bilaleet* (sweet noodles), *humous nakki* (chickpea soup) and *kobs khameer* (bread). At the *cultural lunch (Sun, Tue 1pm, 60 Dh)*, spicy chicken, fish and rice specialities are on the menu.

## CAFÉS

### INSIDERTIP BASTA ARTS CAFÉ
(U C3) (*ψ V4*)

A patio café in one of the restored historic houses in the traditional Bastakiya quarter. Guests are seated on raised Arabian benches or in the European style and enjoy an Arabian or English breakfast, fresh juice, iced mint tea, salads, soups and sandwiches. The little attached shop sells jewellery and art objects. *Daily 10am–10pm | Al-Fahidi Street 63 | Al-Fahidi R/A | tel. 04 3 53 50 71 | Metro: Green Line: Saeediya*

### INSIDERTIP LIME TREE CAFÉ
(109 E2) (*ψ T4*)

The front terrace of this villa is a rendezvous for Europeans who like the snacks, salads, cakes and soups, and meet here for a breakfast-time latte macchiato with crispy croissants. There is a huge choice of freshly pressed juice. *Daily 7.30am–6pm | Jumeirah Road, near the Jumeirah Mosque | tel. 04 3 49 84 98 | www.thelimetreecafe.com | Metro Red Line: Emirates Towers*

### INSIDER TIP ▶ SAHARY GATE
(U C3) (*ill V4*)

In one of the buildings behind the Local House restaurant in Bastakiya a travel agency runs a coffee shop, a souvenir shop and a roof garden, and proprietor Leila Arbouz makes efforts to communicate the culture of the emirates in courses, workshops and exhibitions. *Sat–Thu 9am–8pm, Fri 10am–6pm | Bastakiya House No. 14 | Bur Dubai | tel. 04 3 53 56 60 | www.saharygate.com | Metro Green Line: Saeediya*

### INSIDER TIP ▶ ORGANIC FOODS & CAFÉ
⏱ (109 D4) (*ill S5*)

Organically grown products, fair-trade coffee from Costa Rica, delicious cheese from unpasteurised milk and healthy organic salads: this well-stocked shop attracts European expatriates for shopping and at lunchtime for excellent salads and fruit juices in the café.
*Sun–Wed 10am–10pm, Thu–Sat 10am–midnight | Lower Ground Floor, next to the Waterfront Restaurant | Dubai Mall | tel. 04 4 34 05 77 | www.organicfoodsandcafe.com | Metro Red Line: Dubai Mall*

### INSIDER TIP ▶ SKYVIEW BAR ☀
(U D9) (*ill N3*)

This is the place for high tea in the true sense of the word. Tea-time on the 27th floor of the Burj Al Arab is expensive, but you get a fantastic view with your Darjeeling or Lapsang Souchong. *Bookings for 3pm, 4pm or 5pm | Hotel Burj Al Arab | Jumeirah Road | tel. 04 3 01 76 00 | www.burj-al-arab.com | Metro Red Line: First Gulf Bank*

## ARABIC

### BASTAKIYAH NIGHTS ★
(U C3) (*ill V4*)

Arabian and romantic: in the restored Bastakiya quarter on the Creek flaming torches light the way at night to this restaurant in a historic wind tower house. Arabian food is dished up in eleven rooms on two floors decorated with crafts. In the winter months you can also dine in the courtyard. From the ☀ roof garden there is a view of the Creek and the skyline of Deira. *Daily midday–1am | next to the Ruler's Court | Bastakiya | Bur Dubai | tel. 04 3 53 77 72 | Moderate | Metro Green Line: Saeediya*

### LOCAL HOUSE (U C3) (*ill V4*)
Dishes from the emirates is the strength of this restaurant, which serves authentic regional dishes. *Daily midday–11pm | Al-*

---

★ **Bastakiyah Nights**
A flavour of old Dubai in the historic merchants' quarter: Arabian cooking in the wind tower palace → p. 51

★ **Marina Seafood Restaurant**
Fish served on the pier → p. 53

★ **Bayt al-Wakeel**
Restaurant on a terrace over the Creek with a view of the *abras*, old wooden water taxis → p. 57

★ **Eauzone**
There's no more romantic place to dine in Dubai → p. 52

★ **Magnolia**
Unusual combinations of vegetarian ingredients → p. 54

**MARCO POLO HIGHLIGHTS**

*Fahidi Street 65 | Bastakiya | Bur Dubai | tel. 04 3 53 97 14 | Moderate | Metro Green Line: Saeediya*

### AL-NAFOORAH (109 E3) (⌂ T5)

Al-Nafoorah has several times been voted the best Lebanese restaurant in Dubai thanks to its excellent cooking and a big array of warm and cold starters *(mezze)*.

The classic dish here is *kibbeh nayyehi*, minced lamb with bulgur wheat and mint. The open-air terrace is a really attractive place to dine. *Daily 12.30–5pm and 8pm–midnight | Shopping Boulevard | ground floor of Emirates Towers | tel. 04 3 19 80 88 | www.jumeirahemiratestowers.com | Expensive | Metro Red Line: Emirates Towers*

# GOURMET RESTAURANTS

### Eauzone ★ (U C9) (⌂ K3–Y4)

Sea bream in lemon-and-ginger sauce, risotto with cep mushrooms – everything on the menu here is delicious, and the romantic surroundings enhance the experience: candlelight is reflected in ponds of water, palms swish in the breeze, with the shimmering pool landscape of the Arabian Court Hotel as a backdrop. Three-course menu 450 Dh. *Daily midday–3pm and 7–11pm | Arabian Court | One&Only Royal Mirage | Al-Sufouh Road | Al-Sufouh | tel. 04 3 99 99 99 | www.oneandonlyresorts.com | Metro Red Line: Nakheel*

### Al-Mahara (U D9) (⌂ N 3)

At Captain Nemo's table: access to this restaurant involves a three-minute simulated submarine voyage (in a lift). The table are lined up opposite the glass wall of a large aquarium. The food is expensive, but its quality lives up to the slogan here: 'The finest seafood of the world', and the futuristic surroundings have to be paid for. Booking essential. Three-course menu 700 Dh. *Daily 12.30–2.30pm and 7–23.30pm | Hotel Burj Al Arab | Jumeirah Road | tel. 04 3 01 76 00 | www.burj-al-arab.com | Metro Red Line: First Gulf Bank*

### Ossiano (U C8) (⌂ K–L 1)

For the three-star chef Santi Santamaria no fish is sacred: his Catalan kitchen sends forth such creations as seafood with lobster carpaccio and ravioli made from prawn tails stuffed with wild mushrooms. Diners are seated between walls of glass bricks beneath the eyes of devil rays and groupers *(3-course menu 900 Dh)*. In the same hotel you can also sample the craft of Parisian two-star chef Michel Rostang, in the brasserie. *Daily 7pm–midnight | Atlantis Hotel | Crescent Road | The Palm Jumeirah | tel. 04 4 26 26 26 | www.atlantisthepalm.com | Metro Red Line: Nakheel*

### Verre by Gordon Ramsay (109 D4) (⌂ W5)

Light European haute cuisine: for the selection of dishes and the way they are prepared Gordon Ramsay is consulted, and he regularly comes to Dubai to check that his creations are being cooked properly. Luca Cagliardi, voted the best sommelier in Dubai, is at hand to advise on the choice of wine. Three-course menus 500 Dh. *Sun–Thu 7–11pm | Hilton Dubai Creek | Beniyas Road | tel. 04 2 27 11 11 | www.gordonramsay.com/dubai | Metro Red Line: Al Rigga*

**INSIDER TIP** ▶ **RAVI** (109 F2) (*𝄢 T4*)
Pakistani restaurant mainly catering for Asian men. Wide choice of cheap and tasty *kebabs. Daily 5am–3am | Satwa Road next to R/A | Al-Satwa | tel. 04 3 31 53 53 | Budget | Metro Red Line: Trade Centre*

## SHABESTAN (U D5) (*𝄢 V4*)

The best Persian restaurant in the city: opulent furnishings and traditional Iranian cuisine with live music in the background. For a starter try *houmus* and pitta bread, then rice flavoured with raisins and saffron to go with tender lamb, followed by ice-cream perfumed with rose water, and mocha to finish off. *Daily midday–3pm and 7–11pm | Hotel Radisson BLU, 2nd floor | Baniyas Road | Deira | tel. 04 2 22 71 71 | www.dubai.radissonblu.com | Expensive | Metro Green Line and Red Line: Union*

## FISH RESTAURANTS

### THE FISH MARKET ☆ (U D5) (*𝄢 V4*)

This fish restaurant has been renowned in Dubai for two decades, and it has a simple recipe for success: diners choose the *tiger prawns,* shark steaks or langoustines displayed on an open counter between bamboo and orchids themselves, then select the vegetables and the method of cooking (wok, grilled or fried). Then they wait for the meal to be prepared while enjoying a view of the Creek and a Thai cocktail. *Daily 12.30–3.30 pm and 7.30–11pm | Hotel Radisson BLU, 2nd floor | Baniyas Road | Deira | tel. 04 2 05 70 33 | www.dubai.radissonblu.com | Expensive | Metro Green Line and Red Line: Union*

### MARINA SEAFOOD RESTAURANT ★ ☆ (106 C1) (*𝄢 N4*)

The Jumeirah Beach Hotel's 200-metre (650 ft) pier ends in a modern semi-cir-

A play of light and water: the bar in the Eauzone restaurant

cular building that has a terrific view of the Burj Al Arab and the Jumeirah coast. For a delicious starter try bass sashimi, a Japanese version of carpaccio. In addition to oyster, mussels, prawns and fish, vegetarian dishes are on the menu too. *Daily 7pm–midnight (Fri also 12.30–3pm) | Jumeirah Beach Hotel | Jumeirah Road | tel. 04 3 48 00 00 | www.jumeirah beachhotel.com | Expensive | Metro Red Line: First Gulf Bank*

### PIERCHIC (106 B2) (*𝄢 M4*) ●

The most romantic place to eat sea bass or prawns is beneath the stars: a wooden jetty leads to a terrace built on stilts in the middle of the sea with a stunning view of the illuminated Burj Al Arab and Madinat Jumeirah. Tip: book a table on the terrace! *Daily 1–3pm and 7–11.30pm | Al Qasr | Madinat Jumeirah | Al Sufouh | tel. 04 3 66 88 88 | www.jumeirah.com | Expensive | Metro Red Line: First Gulf Bank*

### SALMONTINI (U D9) (*M5*)

This fish is more what you would expect to eat on a Norwegian fjord than on the Arabian Gulf. Nevertheless, it's worth coming here for smoked heart of salmon, salmon tartar or salmon with pesto – the name of the restaurant tells you what to expect. For dessert try apple pie or sorbet. The entertainment while you eat is a view of the indoor ski hall. *Daily*

# LOW BUDGET

▶ *Karachi Darbar* serves up Pakistani and Indian meals at very low prices. After dark the tables are set up outside. At the *Karama Shopping Complex | Al-Karama |* **(110 B3)** *(M U5) | tel. 04 3 34 74 34 | www.karachidarbar.com | Metro Red Line: Al Karama*

▶ Get 'The Entertainer' coupon book *(250 Dh | www.theentertainerme.com)* to save money when two people dine in selected restaurants, as the second main course is free; there are also coupons for other activities.

▶ In the *Ashwaq Cafeteria (daily 11am–midnight | Sikkat al-Khail Road, opposite the Deira Palace Hotel | (U D2) (M V4) | Deira | tel. 04 2 26 11 64 | Metro Green Line: Al Ras)* you will be served a delicious *shawarma* or lamb, chicken and prawn sandwiches for 4–6 Dh.

*midday–4pm and 8pm–midnight | The Mall of the Emirates, Level 1 (West End) | tel. 04 3 47 58 44 | Moderate | Metro Red Line: Mall of the Emirates*

## FUSION FOOD

### INSIDERTIP FIRE AND ICE
(110 B5) (*M U6*)

The name reveals it: the food here is a play on unexpected contrasts of different tastes, and the brick interior has the atmosphere of a loft in New York. There's more drama to be had watching the chefs at work, especially when the flames shoot up high. Exquisite cooking with a loving attention to detail whether you go for sirloin steak, mashed potato with black truffles or spinach with lemon butter. *Daily 7pm–midnight | Hotel Raffles | Sheikh Rashid Road | Wafi | tel. 04 3 24 88 88 | www.raffles.com | Expensive | Metro Green Line: Healthcare City*

### KEVA (110 B4) (*M U5*)

Dubai's hipsters and up-and-coming people like this place. The dishes are classic modern European combined with Asian spices, ingredients and cooking methods. The welcoming ambience is created through warm earthy tones, lots of wood, Asian art and glass walls encapsulating rose petals. *Daily 11am–3pm | The Lodge | Al-Nasr Leisureland | Oud Metha (behind the American Hospital) | tel. 04 3 34 41 59 | www.keva.ae | Moderate | Metro Green Line: Oud Metha*

### MAGNOLIA ★ ☺ (106 B2) (*M M4*)

The most attractive location in Dubai to indulge in organic vegetarian cuisine. An *abra* takes you across the canals of Madinat Jumeirah to this restaurant and its romantic terrace. Some of the combinations of dishes to form set menus are highly original, and so delicious that even steak fans could get a taste for vegetarian living. Wash it all down wish good wines and glacier water from Greenland. *Wed–Mon 7–11.30pm | Talise Spa | Souk Madinat Jumeirah | tel. 04 3 66 88 88 | www.jumeirah.com | Expensive | Metro Red Line: First Gulf Bank*

### MANHATTAN GRILL (110 B6) (*⬚ U6*)

Businessmen meet here at lunchtime for the three-course set menu, which is very reasonably priced. Fish and lamb specialities feature heavily on the menu. Strawberry crème brûlée is recommended for dessert. *Daily 12.30–3pm and 7–11.30pm (Thu and Fri till 1 am) | Grand Hyatt Hotel | Trade Centre Road | Bur Dubai | tel. 04 3 17 12 34 | www.dubai.grand.hyatt.com | Moderate–Expensive | Metro Green Line: Healthcare City*

### YUM (U D5) (*⬚ V4*)

A popular noodle bar: delicious spicy Asian soups, dim-sum and noodle and seafood dishes in Thai, Indonesian and Malay style prepared in view of the guests. *Daily midday–1am | Hotel Radisson BLU | Baniyas Road | Deira | tel. 04 2 05 73 33 | www.dubai.radissonblu.com | Moderate | Metro Green Line: Baniyas Square*

## INDIAN

### GOVINDA'S (110 C3) (*⬚ U5*)

All-vegetarian dishes, including excellent *dhal* (lentil curry) with spinach; freshly pressed juices are the perfect accompaniment. *Daily midday–3pm and 7pm–midnight (Fri from 1.30pm) | Trade Centre Road, behind the Regent Palace Hotel | Karama | tel. 3 96 00 88 | www.govindasdubai.com | Budget | Metro Red Line: Al-Karama*

### INSIDER TIP ▶ KARANI (U B2) (*⬚ V4*)

Indian families are delighted with the quality here: north Indian food and specialities from Rajasthan, but also classics

The Ashwaq Cafeteria serves cheap and delicious food from a rotating grill

## LOCAL SPECIALITIES

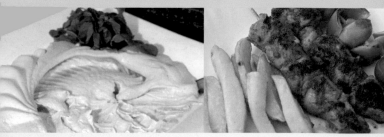

▶ **achar** – vegetables marinated in vinegar and garlic: cauliflower, olives, root vegetables, onions, peppers

▶ **babaganoush** – puree of aubergine and tomato with onions, parsley, salt and sesame oil

▶ **baharat** – a spice mixture containing pepper, coriander, cloves, cumin, nutmeg, cinnamon and paprika

▶ **baklava** – dessert of flaky pastry, almonds, pistachios and cardamom, soaked in honey

▶ **foul medames** – broad beans in a spicy tomato sauce with onions and vegetables

▶ **hammour** – bass from the Arabian Gulf (grilled, fried)

▶ **houmus** – chickpea puree with sesame oil and salt (photo left)

▶ **kebab** – minced meat on a skewer (lamb, beef, sometimes chicken)

▶ **khoubiz** – warm pitta bread used instead of a spoon for meals without cutlery

▶ **labneh** – curd cheese with garlic

▶ **mashwee samak** – grilled fish

▶ **maskoul** – rice with onions

▶ **mehalabiya** – pistachio milk pudding

▶ **muaddas** – rice with brown lentils

▶ **muhammar** – sweet rice with raisins, cardamom, rose water and almonds

▶ **mutabbal** *(moutabel)* – baked aubergines with sesame paste and walnut oil

▶ **qahwa** – coffee (usually with cardamom and no sugar)

▶ **shaurabat adas** – traditional Arabian lentil soup

▶ **shawarma** – thinly sliced lamb or chicken with salad served in pitta bread

▶ **shish kabab** – lamb on a skewer

▶ **shish tawouk** – marinated grilled chicken on a skewer (photo right)

▶ **tabouleh** – salad made from chopped parsley, diced tomato, cucumber, onion, cracked wheat and mint

▶ **wara enab** – vine leaves stuffed with spiced rice

like *dhal* and *raita* (cucumber yoghurt), all of it vegetarian. 16 different kinds of *naan* bread are on offer, and much-loved *gulab jamun* (circular, deep-fried cakes soaked in syrup) round off the meal. *Daily midday–11pm | Al-Bahama Street 312 (behind Al-Fa-hidi Street) | Bur Dubai | tel. 04 3 53 06 70 | Budget | Metro: Green Line: Saeediya*

### LUCKY (U C3) (🗺 V4)

Since 1958 Indian, Chinese and Mongolian dishes have been served here to diners on a low budget, nowadays in clean and decent surroundings on the first floor with plastic tablecloths and serviettes. Recommended dishes include tasty *alu mutter* and *palak paneer,* two Indian vegetarian dishes with potatoes and peas or spinach and cheese, plus they also do a classic *chicken tikka. Daily 11.30am–4pm and 7–11.45pm | Al-Fahidi Street, opposite the Al-Musalla Post Office | Meena Bazar | Bur Dubai | tel. 04 3 53 45 63 | Budget | Metro Green Line: Saeediya*

## RESTAURANTS WITH A VIEW

**INSIDER TIP APPLE ● (U D5) (⩔ W4)**
This eatery offers a wide selection of dishes, mainly Arab. The Lebanese buffet is a good choice, and everything is reasonably priced. From the ☼ outside terrace you have an impressive view of the comings and goings on the Dubai Creek. And what about smoking a *shisha* instead of dessert? *Daily 8am–midnight | Twin Towers Shopping Centre, 3rd floor | Baniyas Road | Deira | tel. 04 2 27 44 46 | Budget | Metro Green Line: Baniyas Square*

## BAYT AL-WAKEEL ★ (U B2) (⩔ V4)
This traditional merchant's house with its two-storey arcades serves snacks and Arabian dishes, including delicious fish specialities, on a ☼ large wooden terrace above the Creek. *Daily midday–midnight | Bur Dubai Souk (between the abra docks) | Bur Dubai | tel. 04 3 53 05 30 | Moderate | Metro Green Line: Al-Ghubaiba*

## AL-DAWAAR ☼ (U F2) (⩔ W4)
If you get a table in the front row, all of Dubai is at your feet, as this restaurant on the 25th floor of the Hyatt Regency Hotel rotates 360° every hour. The ori-

ental and European buffet is so exquisite that you will need at least two full rotations to try all you want. À la carte orders

Exquisite fish: Al-Dawaar leaves nothing to be desired

are also taken. It's highly recommended to book a table at the window! *Daily 12.30–3.30pm and 7pm–midnight | Hyatt Regency Hotel | Al-Khaleej Road | Deira | tel. 04 3 17 22 22 | www.dubai.regency.hyatt.com | Expensive | Metro Green Line: Palm Deira*

## KAN ZAMAN ☼ (U C1) (⩔ V4)
Romantic and bustling at one and the same time: you sit outdoors at one of the many tables set up along the broad Creek promenade in front of the Heritage & Diving Village. The menu features international and Lebanese dishes; the mixed grill is particularly good. Finish off with Moroccan mint tea and a puff at a shisha. *Daily 11am–1am | Shindagha | Bur Dubai | tel. 04 3 93 99 13 | Moderate | Metro Green Line: Al Ghubaiba*

# SHOPPING

**WHERE TO START?**

The shops selling the famous designers are situated on Fashion Avenue in the Dubai Mall, the world's second-largest mall, which you can reach by taking the Metro to the **Dubai Mall** stop (Red Line). In this modern shopping nirvana you will also find electronic goods and the latest young fashion. For oriental bazaar atmosphere try the **Souk al-Bahar** opposite, where good-quality Arabian souvenirs are sold. If you enjoy browsing in traditional bazaars, the **Bur Dubai Souk** between the abra docks on Creek Bur Dubai is a good option.

**Shopaholics say with a grin that Dubai should really be spelled 'Do buy'. And critical voices claim that spectacular new monuments to the consumer society have taken the place of other monuments or sights in the emirate.**

And indeed shopping is one of the main reasons to take a trip to Dubai, where the opportunities to spend money are simply inexhaustible. Whatever your taste, you will find the bargain you are looking for. If you seek oriental products such as spices and perfumed oils, the alleyways of the souks, the traditional Arabian bazaars, have it all. Designer fashion can be found in the numerous shopping malls – and it's a good deal cheaper there than in Europe. The range of electronics is great, and for jewellery, especially gold,

## Dubai is shopping heaven: in traditional souks and glittering new retail temples there is something for every taste

Dubai is Aladdin's cave. Indian tailors are specialised in making suits and women's clothes to order within a few days. The pashmina scarves that are on offer everywhere are a low-price item to take back home. They are made from a wide variety of fabrics, not actually always from cashmere or silk.

The relaxed atmosphere when you take a shopping trip is extremely pleasant. Everywhere you can inspect the goods and make comparisons without the traders and sales assistants pressing you to buy

and quoting 'best prices' unasked. In Dubai the prices are fixed. The exception to this rule are the souks, where haggling is usual. The traders there will often reduce their prices by a third if you take your time over bargaining with them.

The luxurious shopping malls are part and parcel of the Dubai experience. They are architectural showpieces, fitted out with granite and marble, not to mention genuine palm trees. There is even an annual festival dedicated to retail indulgence: for the four-week-long *Dubai*

*Shopping Festival,* when many discounts are offered and prize draws held, the whole city gives itself over to shopping fever *(see p. 91 | Jan/Feb | www.mydsf.ae).*

are known only to experts in the West. The star of the local scene is the Iranian artist Farhad Moshiri, whose works seem to viewers like a synthesis of Arab calligraphy and neo-Baroque. *Sat–Thu 11am–*

The Majlis Gallery presents paintings with regional themes in extremely pretty surroundings

## ART

**MAJLIS GALLERY (U C3) (∅ V4)**
Changing exhibitions of the works of local artists and international painters who have some artistic connection to the region. *Sat–Thu 10am–1pm and 4–7pm | Al-Fahidi Street 67 | Al-Fahidi R/A | www.themajlisgallery.com | Metro Green Line: Saeediya*

**INSIDER TIP THE THIRD LINE**
**(107 D3) (∅ N5)**
Dubai's most famous gallery, housed in a building that has a plain appearance seen from outside, represents contemporary artists from Arabia and Iran who

*8pm | Sheikh Zayed Road between Interchanges 3 and 4 (near The Courtyard) | Al-Qoz 3 | www.thethirdline.com | Metro Red Line: First Gulf Bank*

**INSIDER TIP XVA GALLERY**
**(U C3) (∅ V4)**
In this renovated house with a wind tower most of the works on display are by modern Arabian artists. Shop and café attached. *Sat–Thu 9am–7pm, Fri 10am–5pm | Al-Fahidi Street, behind the Majlis Gallery | Bastakiya | www.xvagallery.com | Metro Red Line: Saeediya*

## SHOPPING MALLS

Dubai has taken the idea of the shopping mall to extremes. The 40 or so of them are shopping centres and theme parks all in one. People don't go to a mall only for shopping, but to be entertained as well. Cinemas, aquariums, ski slopes, ice rinks and an overwhelming number of cafés and restaurants pull in the crowds. The other factor is Dubai's climate: from May to September life is bearable only in air-conditioned rooms. The shopping malls are also just the job if you are looking for shoes, clothes for children, fashion accessories, delicatessen, beauty products and underwear.

### BURJUMAN CENTRE (U A5) (*ω V5*)

An exclusive mall with 300 shops, including Burberry, Calvin Klein, Cartier, Chanel, Dolce & Gabbana, Ferragamo, Max Mara, Prada and Saks Fifth Avenue. For the hip styles go to Diesel, Zara and Quiksilver. To recover: 20 cafés, a food court and several restaurants. *Sat–Thu 10am–10pm, Fri 2–10pm | Trade Centre Road/Khalid Bin al-Waleed Road | www.burjuman.com | Metro Red Line: Khalid Bin Al-Waleed*

### DEIRA CITY CENTRE (111 D5) (*ω W6*)

Debenhams and Woolworths are the favourite addresses in Dubai's oldest mall, which scores with its transparent architecture. It is home to 300 boutiques (from Burberry to Zegna), various cafés (including no less than three Starbucks), a food court and several restaurants, cinemas and a Magic Planet (where you can play video games or try the flight simulator). A further plus is that Deira City Centre runs ● four free shuttle bus routes from many hotels in Dubai. *Sun–Wed 10am–10pm, Thu–Sat 10am–midnight | Baniyas Road/Al-Ittihad Road (near the Floating Bridge) | Deira | www.deiracitycentre.com | Metro Red Line: Deira City Centre*

### DUBAI DUTY FREE (111 E6) (*ω W6–Y7*)

The last temptation before your onward flight or return home: this retail space of 10,000 m² in the Sheikh Rashid Terminal, which has been extended several times to the point where shoppers can get lost, turns over 1 billion US dollars per year in a host of little boutiques and larger stores that sell designer fashion, gold jewellery, leather goods, cosmetics, sports equipment and electronic goods from all over the world – some of it at attractive prices. *www.dubaidutyfree.com | Metro Red Line: Airport*

### DUBAI MALL ★ (109 D4) (*ω S5*)

Luxury and opulence are the hallmarks of Dubai's biggest mall, which is the world's second-largest. Galleries, arcades, floors inlaid with shining marble and granite, works of art, splashing fountains and effects with light and water are the frame-

★ **Dubai Mall**
The world's second-largest mall draws customers with shopping of the highest order and a number of other superlatives → p. 61

★ **Souk Al-Bahar**
Arab design, top location. Come here for high-class souvenirs → p. 64

★ **Gold Souk**
All that glitters here is gold. The low wages of the people who make the jewellery ensure that you can buy high-quality goods at low prices in Dubai → p. 65

**MARCO POLO HIGHLIGHTS**

work for a retail area amounting to 220 000 m². Interactive information screens make it easy to find your way around. Over 1200 shops cater for every wish. Book World by Kinokuniya, for example, a branch of a Japanese chain of bookshops, is phenomenal. The lower floor harbours the Gold Souk, where some 300 jewellers' shops twinkle beneath a starry dome. Go to the first floor for a branch of the French high-class department store Galeries Lafayette (18 000 m²), or to Fashion Avenue for boutiques run by all the designers who matter. This mall's biggest attraction is the ● Dubai Aquarium, which you can admire from various vantage points in the complex. *Daily 10am–midnight | Doha Street, from Sheikh Zayed Road, 1st Interchange | www.*

## LOW BUDGET

▶ What you see is what you get here! Low-cost souvenirs, imitations of designer T-shirts, jeans, copies of leather bags and wristwatches: all to be had at *Blue Marine (Sat–Thu 9am–10pm, Fri 9–11 am and 4–10pm | Karama Shopping Centre | (114 B3) (ᗡ U5) | Bur Dubai | Metro Red Line: Al-Karama)*.

▶ Half-price shishas, second-hand books, used designer clothing and English china: all on sale at the *Dubai Flea Market,* to the sounds of local bands. *Nov–April 1st Sat of the month 9am–3pm | Safa Park Gate 5 | Al-Safa (between Sheikh Zayed Road and Al-Wasl Road) | (112 B3) (ᗡ Q4) | admission 3 Dh | www.dubai-fleamarket.com | Metro Red Line: Business Bay*

*thedubaimall.com | Metro Red Line: Dubai Mall*

### FESTIVAL CENTRE (114 C2) (ᗡ V7)
Come here if you want to meet Europeans who are shopping at Ikea. A huge glass dome rises above 370 shops with a view of the city's high-rise skyline from the ☀ upper floors. The best place to drink your mango shake is one of the cafés outside the mall on the canal *(Canal Walk, Festival Waterfront)*. Little electric *abras* ply its waters. *Daily 10am–midnight | Festival City | www.festivalcentre. com | Metro Green Line: Festival City*

### AL-GHURAIR CENTRE (U F6) (ᗡ W5)
This is the classic mall, Dubai's oldest and at the same time the first modern shopping mall on the Arabian Peninsula. Owned by the Al Ghurair family (according to the Forbes list among the world's 100 richest), this mall is not the latest thing in architectural terms but has been given a thorough refurbishing and attracts lots of regular customers from the Gulf states. Many famous international fashion designers (Givenchy, Dior) are represented here, as well as more recent brands (Esprit, Guess, Mexx), and what may be the biggest choice of perfumeries has gathered under its roof. *Sat–Thu 10am–10pm, Fri 2–10pm | Al-Riqqa St. | Deira | www.alghuraircity.com | Metro Green Line and Red Line: Union Square*

### INSIDER TIP IBN BATTUTA MALL
(U C9) (ᗡ Q4)
What distinguishes this mall from the others in Dubai are the elaborate illusions of its architecture: visitors stroll through the lands that the great Arab seafarer Ibn Battuta saw on his travels in the 14th century: Persia, India, China, Egypt. Galleries are dedicated to these countries and kitted out in the style of

Shops, cafés, a hotel, entertainment for children – fun all round in the Dubai Mall

village streets and squares with rows of houses in the Arabian style, including domed buildings, mosaic-clad walls and huge, antique-looking sailing ships. Few of the 290 shops are in the hands of de-signer brands, but to compensate there is a good assortment of Arabian crafts. 70 restaurants and cafés (including a food court) take care of the culinary side. A recommended eatery is the Indian restaurant *Mumbai Sé* in the *India Court* *(tel. 04 3 66 98 55 | www.mumbai-se. com | Moderate)*. *Sun–Wed 10am–10pm, Thu–Sat 10am–midnight | Sheikh Zayed Road, between Interchanges 5 and 6 | Je-bel Ali | www.ibnbattutamall.com | Metro Red Line: Ibn Battuta*

## MALL OF THE EMIRATES
(U D9) (*M5*)

The operators of the world's third-largest shopping mall describe it as a 'shopping resort', because lovers of the retail expe-rience can not only buy things here but can also stay – right next door at the five-star Kempinski Hotel. Not only that, but this mall is connected with *Ski Dubai (see p. 45)*. In the area of the front entrance you can even get a glimpse of the ski slopes through a window and plan your visit to the mall over a glass of tea.

Among the 466 shops there is a branch of London's upmarket Harvey Nichols department store, as well as boutiques selling Missoni and Marc Jacobs. Dozens of cafés and restaurants cater for this mall, and for older children and teenagers there are rides such as dodgems in the *Magic Planet* indoor amusement park. At regular intervals shuttle buses fetch customers from luxury hotels (e.g. the Ritz-Carlton and Royal Mirage on Jumeirah Beach). *Sun–Wed 10am–10pm, Thu–Sat 10am–midnight | Sheikh Zayed Road, between Interchanges 4 and 5 | www.malloftheemirates.com | Metro Red Line: Mall of the Emirates*

### INSIDER TIP MERCATO TOWN CENTRE
(109 D2) *(𝛺 S4)*

Italy is the theme here, with recreations of the atmosphere of Venice and a piazza. This medium-sized mall (90 shops and six restaurants) aims its expensive offerings at the expatriates living on Jumeirah Road. The air-conditioned interior reflects the style of the Italian Renaissance with its bridges, lanes and façades. *Sun–Wed 10am–10pm, Thu–Sat 10am–midnight | Jumeirah Beach Road | www.mercatotowncentre.com | Metro Red Line: Dubai Mall*

### SOUK AL-BAHAR ★ ☼ ●
(109 D4) *(𝛺 S5)*

This is one of the newest shopping complexes, its architecture and styling done in a genuinely Arabian manner with oriental arcades and winding corridors on two levels housing 100 boutiques plus 22 cafés and restaurants. Greenery in the shape of palms and big copper lamps from Marrakech add to the mood of oriental magic.

The location of the Souk Al-Bahar is also unusual: in the middle of *The Old Town Island*, which is surrounded by the *Dubai Lake*, a waterway next to the Burj Khalifa. Lots of well-attended cafés and restaurants lie directly beside the water. The souk affords a view of the *Burj Khalifa*, Dubai's architectural icon, and

also has direct access to the *Dubai Mall*. The luxury hotel *The Palace of The Old Town,* which lives up to its name and can be admired from inside, is also part of this complex. *Sat–Thu 10am–10pm, Fri 2–10pm | Old Town Island, Sheikh Zayed Road, 1st Interchange | Downtown Dubai | Metro Red Line: Dubai Mall*

### WAFI CITY MALL (110 B5) *(𝛺 U6)*

Gigantic pyramid architecture of glass, chrome and steel, visible from afar, is the unique selling proposition of this mall, which is highly regarded by the local Emiratis (voted 'best shopping mall' recently). Wafi encompasses 300 shops (the list includes Marks & Spencer, Chanel, Gant, Jaeger-LeCoultre, Laurel, Missoni, Miss Sixty, Oilily, Qui and Strenesse) and about 30 restaurants and cafés, where the quality is high. A further attraction is the Arabian *Souk Khan Murjan* on the lower level. Its 150 stores across two floors are devoted to Islamic-inspired crafts and Arabian jewellery, carpets and furniture. *Sun–Wed 10am–10pm, Thu–Sat 10am–midnight | Oud Metha Road (from Sheikh Zayed Road) | Wafi | www.wafi.com | Metro Green Line: Healthcare City*

## SOUKS

### INSIDER TIP GOLD & DIAMOND PARK
(106 B3) *(𝛺 N5)*

90 jewellery boutiques and over 100 manufacturers provide a comprehensive view of the art of manufacturing jewellery. The *museum gallery* presents details of working methods, and also exhibits precious items of Arabian and Indian design. Several cafés, a patio and a restaurant are on site. *Sat–Thu 10am–10pm, Fri 4–10pm | Sheikh Zayed Road, Interchange 4 | Al-Quoz | www.goldanddiamondpark.com | Metro Red Line: First Gulf Bank*

### GOLD SOUK ⭐ (U D2) (*ᗰ V4*)

The United Arab Emirates import 300 tons of gold each year. Part of this enormous quantity is transformed into jewellery by cheap Asian labour. In the Gold Souk one shop is lined up next to another. Gold items (22 and 24 carat) are sold by weight for low prices, as the customer pays hardly anything to meet the costs of working the metal. The designs tend to be showy, corresponding to Indian taste. Those looking around for something in the European style may be disappointed. The best time to come here is after dark, when the lanes fill up and Arab customers drop in, ladies escorted by their husbands and accompanied by the children and their Asian nannies. *Daily 9.30am–1pm and 4–10pm | Al-Ras Street | Deira | Metro Green Line: Al Ras* 24-carat gold items, if desired in Cartier and Bulgari designs, can be found at the larger jewellers' stores in every shopping mall.

### TRADITIONAL SOUKS

Today Dubai's traditional souks largely have the character of shopping streets in which countless shops display wares of a similar kind.

In the *Textile Souk (also known as the Bur Dubai Souk, between the abra docks on the Creek in Bur Dubai,* (U B–C2) (*ᗰ V4*)) the goods are of course fabrics.

In the *Spice Souk* (Al-Ras Street, Deira (U C2) (*ᗰ V4*)) exotic spices from Asia and Arabia are sold in packages or from huge jute sacks at prices lower than in the supermarkets.

The *Perfume Souk* in the street named Sikkat al-Khail (Deira (U D2) (*ᗰ V4*)) has oriental scented oils and perfumes that customers can mix themselves.

Gold Souk: glittering jewellery in extravagant designs

# ENTERTAINMENT

**CITY WHERE TO START?**

Dubai has no 'Bermuda triangle' for party people to disappear into. But a good place to start is **Madinat Jumeirah**: have a drink in one of the upscale bars of the souk of the same name – the Madinat Rooftop would be a good choice – and move on to one of the district's hip dance clubs towards midnight. **Dubai Marina** also has trendy nightlife: expatriates hang out in Bar 44, while the Buddha Bar is more for businessmen. In the shopping boulevard of the **Emirates Towers** Harry Ghatto's pulls in cool locals of the younger generation, and at Vu's Bar there's a mix of Emiratis and tourists.

**Internationally sought-after DJs, rock stars and pop idols perform in Dubai. You can party through the night any day of the week, but most of the action happens between Thursday and Saturday.**

Paul Van Dyk in the Madinat Arena, D12 and Goldfish in The Lodge, Queen in the Festival Centre Mall – in Dubai night owls are well catered for, and at fairly reasonable cost. Concert tickets, for example, cost much less than in Europe. On the other hand, drinks are nowhere more expensive than in Dubai's clubs. Here they will charge you 5000 dirham for a magnum of champagne without anyone raising an eyebrow, and in the Skyview Bar a whisky cocktail can set you back 7500 dollars.

Photo: Al-Shindagha waterfront

**From a shisha café to a dinner cruise –
choose between traditional evening
entertainment, hip bars and clubbing**

Dubai is also paradise for women who like going out. Even amongst the western expats there is a significant surplus of men, so on 'ladies night' (usually Tuesday) bars and nightclubs do all they can to tempt them in with special offers such as free admission and free drinks.

To get up to speed with what's going on in the bars, dance clubs, night clubs, karaoke bars and music clubs, get hold of TimeOut Dubai, which comes out every week and is available in shopping malls, bookshops and hotels or at newspaper stands.

Watch out for one special feature of Dubai nightlife: in the month of Ramadan, so-called Ramadan tents *(ifthar)* open each day after dark offering an opulent buffet, entertainment, folklore and shishas.

From 6pm onwards, bars and dance clubs admit only persons over 21 years of age. Some bars do a check on every guest. It's important to note one thing: anyone who appears to be drunk in public runs the risk of arrest.

## BARS

### 360° ★ ⚘ (106 C1) (*M N4*)

From 5pm well-to-do expats meet for a sundowner, and by 10pm the chic and beautiful people are clinking glasses filled with champagne cocktails. The bar has a unique location above the sea with a view of the changing colours of the Burj Al Arab and the starry sky. Cool lounge furnishings, beanbags as seats and shishas all contribute to the relaxed and classy atmosphere; on Friday evenings this is a hip place to meet – and

Burj Al Arab: even more spectacular at night than by day

packed. *Daily from 5pm | Jumeirah Beach Hotel | Jumeirah Road | Metro Red Line: First Gulf Bank*

### BAR 44 ⚘ (104 C1) (*M J4*)

Romantic and just the thing for couples: from as high up as this, the view looks even better by candlelight with live piano music. *Sat–Wed 6pm–2am, Thu 6pm–3am | Grosvenor House, 44th floor | West Marina Beach | Dubai Marina | www.grosvenorhouse-dubai.com | Metro Red Line: Dubai Marina*

### INSIDER TIP ▶ BARASTI BAR
(104 C1) (*M K3*)

A touch of the Caribbean: European visitors and residents love this beach bar in a top location on a pier in Dubai Marina; you sit beneath a canopy of palm fronds or on carpets under the sky, drink a beer or order a cocktail. *Daily 11am–1.30am | Le Meridien Mina Seyahi Beach Resort & Marina | Al-Sufouh Road | Dubai Marina | www.lemeridien.com/minaseyahi | Metro Red Line: Dubai Marina*

### BUDDHA BAR ★ (104 C1) (*M J3*)

Love and compassion in Dubai – this theme, imported from Paris, goes down well in the desert too. Specially made New Age compilations with Asian influences are played in the lounge and bar, and a Zen restaurant is part of it all. Not to mention the view of the marina and an enormous statue of Buddha. *Daily 8pm–2am | Hotel Grosvenor House | West Marina Beach | Dubai Marina | tel. 04 3 99 88 88 | www.grosvenorhouse-dubai.com | Metro Red Line: Dubai Marina*

### CHILLOUT (106 C–D3) (*M O5*) ●

Dubai's coolest bar. Everything is made of ice, several feet thick: the seats, tables, walls and bar are frozen. The atmosphere is reminiscent of a Star Wars film, which is partly down to the fluorescent lighting. In the acclimatisation room, guests slip into padded jackets and gloves before entering the bar at minus six degrees Celsius (°F 21). No more than 45 people are allowed in at a time, to avoid their body heat raising the room temperature. Once inside they can definitely chill out, whether with alcohol-free cocktails or hot chocolate. *Daily 10am–10pm, Thu/Fri 10am–midnight | Times Square Center | Sheikh Zayed Road, between Interchange 3 and 4 | www.chilloutatdubai.com | admission 60 Dh, Metro Red Line: Al-Quoz*

## CIGAR BAR (109 F3) (*ØØ T5*)

Although Dubai has had a smoking ban indoors since 2008, aficionados of cigars can indulge their passion with Montecristo, Cohiba and top brands from Cuba. *Daily 6pm–2am | Fairmont Hotel, 2nd floor | Sheikh Zayed Road | www.fairmont. com/dubai | Metro Red Line: Trade Centre*

## INSIDER TIP HARRY GHATTO'S
(109 E3) (*ØØ T5*)

Karaoke bar in the Tokyo Restaurant, with changing themes and 1000 songs. For anyone who feels shy, there's also a microphone at the bar, and the waiters will show you how to do your stuff on the stage. *Daily 8pm–3am | Emirates Towers, Shopping Boulevard, 1st floor | Sheikh Zayed Road | Metro Red Line: Emirates Towers*

## LOTUS ONE (109 F3) (*ØØ T5*)

Thai-style restaurant bar with its own DJ and music at a civilised volume; sometimes live music too. *Daily midday–3am | Convention Centre Tower in the World Trade Centre, ground floor | Sheikh Zayed Road, next to the Novotel Hotel | www. lotus1.com | Metro Red Line: Trade Centre*

## ROOFTOP BAR ☽ (105 D1) (*ØØ K 3–4*)

Many people think this is the most romantic spot in Dubai: candles, seating on oriental cushions and high-class lounge furnishings on the roof terrace of a luxury hotel, the Royal Mirage; beneath the stars and high above Jumeirah Beach you can sip cocktails while listening to cool rhythms. *Daily 5.30pm–1am | Arabian Court of the Royal Mirage Hotel | Al-Sufouh Road | http://royalmirage.one-andonlyresorts.com | Metro Red Line: Nakheel*

## SKYVIEW BAR ☽ (U D9) (*ØØ N3*)

A view to die for of *The Palm* and the coast from a height of 650 ft; this place sets its sights on rich customers: the drink called '27,321' costs 7500 US dollars – it's Scotch served in a glass of 18-carat gold. New cocktails can be created individually for each guest in the mobile trolley bar by the *mixologist*. *Daily midday–2am, booking essential | Burj Al Arab, 27th floor | Jumeirah Road | tel. 04 3 0176 00 | www.burj-al-arab.com | Metro Red Line: First Gulf Bank*

---

★ **360°**
High above the sea, everyday life seems miles away → p. 68

★ **Buddha Bar**
New Age music and a little bit of that Zen feeling → p. 68

★ **Dinner in the desert**
Action and romance outside the city → p. 71

★ **Dinner cruise on a dhow**
… and the city skyline glides gently past → p. 72

**MARCO POLO HIGHLIGHTS**

## CINEMA

**VU'S BAR** 🌿 **(109 E3)** *(𝄞 T5)*

Two lifts zoom up to the modern minimalist-style bar on the 51st floor. There is a fantastic view from the sea all the way to the desert. 200 (!) classic cocktails including those that pack an alcoholic punch like Long Island Iced Tea and newcomers like Fraisini (pink champagne with strawberry puree). *Daily midday–3am | Emirates Towers Hotel, 51st floor | Sheikh Zayed Road | www.jumeirahemiratestowers.com | Metro Red Line: Emirates Towers*

### CINEMA

Dubai has a number of multiplex cinemas with up to two dozen screens each. Most films are shown in English, and tickets cost 20–30 Dh. To give a varied population what it wants, all sorts of international films are on the schedule, including Bollywood productions (in Hindi too). *CineStar (Deira City Centre | tel. 04 2 94 90 00), CineStar (The Mall of the Emirates | tel. 04 3 41 42 22), Grand Cinecity (Al-Ghurair City | tel. 04 2 28 98 98), Grand (Festival City | tel. 04 2 32 83 28), Grand (Mercato Town Centre | tel. 04 3 49 97 13)*

### DANCE CLUBS

**INSIDER TIP ▶ CHI AT THE LODGE**
**(110 B4)** *(𝄞 U5)*

Outdoor disco: the Balinese-style *Chi Garden* organises hip and modern fancy-dress parties. *Daily 7pm–3am | Chi Garden, The Lodge, Al-Nasr Leisureland (behind the American Hospital) | Oud Metha | www.lodgedubai.com | Metro Green Line: Healthcare City*

**INSIDER TIP ▶ SANCTUARY**
**U C8)** *(𝄞 K–L2)*

Dubai's superclub: resident DJ Frederick Stone likes soul and funk with a touch of Chicago house. The main room can hold

# CAMEL & HORSE RACES

There is a long tradition of camel racing, and even if today the jockeys that 'ride' the dromedaries are robots, Emiratis are still passionately attached to this pastime. Those who don't have a camel in the race themselves can enjoy the contest as spectators and roar their support for the animals. The winners carry off big prize money. Dubai and the other emirates all have their own camel racetracks, which are outside the cities in the middle of the desert. Tourists are always welcome. *Al-Marmoum Camel Race Track | (0) (𝄞 0) | Al-Ain Road (E66, 25 mi east of Dubai, beyond The Seven's Rugby Complex and Esso petrol station on the right) | Oct–March Thu–Sat, training from 7.30 am, races from 2.30pm | free admission*

Horse races, most of which have thoroughbred Arab horses competing, are also a major event. The atmosphere is international, as the locals are joined by expatriates from all over the world who want to see these remarkable animals. *Meydan Race Course | (116 C2) (𝄞 R–S8) | Al-Meydan Street | Nad al-Sheba (6 mi southeast of the centre, from Al-Ain Road or Sheikh Zayed Road 2nd Interchange) | Nov–March Thu and Fri 7pm | admission 85 Dh | www.meydan.ae*

What could be more romantic? Dinner Cruise on the Creek

up to 2000 guests, and VIPs in their private suites look down onto the dance floor. Another room for 500 puts the focus on R&B. When you need a spot of fresh air, there's a terrace with a fountain. *Daily 9.30pm–3am | Atlantis Hotel | Crescent Road | The Palm Jumeirah | www.atlantisthepalm.com | Metro Red Line: Nakheel*

**INSIDER TIP ▶ TRIBE** (109 E3) (*∅ T5*)
Ultra-chic women got up to the nines and their free-spending partners come here on Wednesdays for the Persiana Night, when Iranian DJs put on Persian underground music, funky house and old favourites from the 80s. *Daily 10pm–3am | Crowne Plaza Dubai | Sheikh Zayed Road | www.tribe-club.com | Metro Red Line: Emirates Towers*

## DINNER SPECIALS

### DINNER IN THE DESERT ★
Watch the sun go down from the top of a sand dune and then dine under the stars – now that's an experience that no visitor to Dubai should miss. The procedure doesn't vary much: a 4WD accommodating 4–6 passengers picks you up in the afternoon at the hotel and takes you into the desert, up and down across the crests of dunes that can be over 300 ft high. When it gets dark, it's time to go to the Bedouin camp. Here, in the middle of the desert, an Arabian buffet with specialities from the grill is prepared. You sit on oriental carpets, while music is played and belly dancers work their magic. There is also an opportunity to ride a camel or order a shisha. Around 10pm the Jeep takes you back to the hotel.

Packages including pick-up from the hotel *(120–180 Dh per person)* are on offer from all the city's travel agents, e.g. *Oasis Palm Tourism (Riqqa Road | Deira | tel. 04 2 62 99 93 | www.opdubai.com)* or *Arabian Adventures (Emirates Holidays Building, 1st floor | Sheikh Zayed Road | tel. 04 3 43 99 66 | www.arabian-adventures.*

Cooz: listen to jazz and sip a cocktail with Hitchcock to keep an eye on you

com | *Metro Red Line: Jumeirah Lake Towers).*

## DINNER CRUISE ✴

Gaily illuminated ★ ● dhows sail from the mouth to the end of the Creek. First you enjoy a sundowner on the upper deck, then dinner on the air-conditioned deck below, where an extensive buffet with Arabian and international dishes is laid on. The sight of night-time Dubai gliding past is a good reason to go back to the upper deck to puff on a shisha. The boats can be found on the Deira side between the Radisson BLU *(Al-Mansour | tel. 04 2 05 70 33)* and the Sheraton Hotel *(Metro: Union)* or in Bur Dubai on Al-Seef Road *(Danat | tel. 04 3 51 11 17 | Metro: Khalid Bin Al Waleed)* and in the Al-Boom Tourist Village *(tel. 04 3 43 30 00 | Metro: Healthcare City).* Prices: 150–200 Dh per person.

A more expensive version, modern with all-round glazing, is *Bateaux Dubai (Al-Seef Road | tel. 04 3 99 49 94 | www.bateauxdubai.com | 325 Dh | Metro Green Line: Saeediya).* A further operator: *www.creekcruises.com*

## JAZZ

### BLUE BAR (109 F3) (*ω T5*)

Despite the name, they play more jazz than blues here. Guests can keep an eye on everything from a high stool or loll around on a comfy sofa. *Daily 2pm–2am | Novotel Hotel, ground floor | Sheikh Zayed Road, behind the World Trade Centre | Metro Red Line: Trade Centre*

### INSIDER TIP ▶ COOZ (110 B6) (*ω U6*)

Repeatedly voted one of the best bars. Intimate cocktail lounge with a jazz pianist and singer. *Daily 6pm–3am | Grand Hyatt Hotel | Al Qutaeyat Road | www.dubai.grand.hyatt.com | Metro Green Line: Al-Jaddaf*

**UP ON THE TENTH** 🍸 (U D5) (𝄞 V4)

A favourite with jazz lovers: intimate and romantic, and up on the 10th floor there is an uninterrupted view of the Creek. A changing roll call of jazz musicians perform, sometimes for a solo piano evening. *Daily 6.30pm–2am | Radisson BLU-Hotel, 10th floor | Beniyas Road Deira | www.dubai.radissonblu.com | Metro Green Line and Red Line: Union Square*

## PUBS

**FIBBER MAGEE'S** (109 F3) (𝄞 T5)

Visitors from Ireland might not be convinced by this imitation of a Dublin pub, but the Guinness is on draught and sport, mainly football, is shown on the TV screen. At lunchtime they dish up INSIDER TIP reasonably price food, some of it Irish. *Daily midday–1am | between the Crowne Plaza and Fairmont Hotel at the back | Sheikh Zayed Road | www.fibbersdubai.com | Metro Red Line: Trade Centre*

INSIDER TIP **IRISH VILLAGE** (111 D6) (𝄞 V6)

A green lawn and Irish beer on draught: the Irish community comes here for all sorts of events, and many other expats like to join them. English and Irish visiting musicians often perform here. *Daily 11am–1.30am | Aviation Club | Al-Garhoud Road (north of the Garhoud Bridge next to the Tennis Stadium) | www.theirishvillage. ae | Metro Red Line: GGICO (Garhoud)*

## THEATRE

**DUBAI COMMUNITY THEATRE & ARTS CENTRE (DUCTAC)** (U D9) (𝄞 M5)

Dubai's non-profit organisation puts on a big range of art exhibitions and performances all year round, ranging from Disney's High School Musical, live on stage, to performances by touring British chamber orchestras and 'Sing Star' karaoke competitions for school kids. *The Mall of the Emirates, Level 2 | Al-Barsha | tel. 04 3 41 47 77 | www.ductac.org | Metro Red Line: Mall of the Emirates*

## WINE BARS

**CIN CIN** (109 F3) (𝄞 T5)

This horseshoe-shaped wine bar has an avant-garde style decor and a legendary wine cellar where 350 fine and famous vintages are stored. Savour them to the sound of European dance music or soul. *Daily 6pm–2am | Fairmont Hotel | Sheikh Zayed Road | www.fairmont.com/dubai | Metro Red Line: Trade Centre*

INSIDER TIP **VINTAGE** (110 B5) (𝄞 U6)

Intimate living-room atmosphere, candle-lit, with couches and armchairs. Various appetisers are served with the wine. *Fri–Wed 6pm–1am, Thu 4pm–2am | The Pyramids | Wafi | Metro Green Line: Healthcare City*

# LOW BUDGET

▶ Admission is free to the evening events and folklore performances in the *Heritage & Diving Village* in Bur Dubai → p. 30

▶ ● ‚Movies under the Stars' is the motto on Sunday nights on the roof of the Wafi Mall; vintage films are screened, with free admission! *Oct–May Sun 8pm–midnight | Rooftop Gardens, entrance next to Mahi Mahi Restaurant and through the Thai Chi Restaurant | tel. 04 3 24 41 00 | Wafi Mall | Oud Metha Road | (114 B5) (𝄞 U6) | www.wafi.com | Metro Green Line: Healthcare City*

# WHERE TO STAY

**Dubai has about 350 hotels with 41,000 rooms and 165 apartment hotels with 15,000 apartments; new ones are being built all the time, and even more are planned.**

Despite the huge number of beds, the capacity utilisation in Dubai is extremely high: 81 per cent according to official figures. This causes prices, which are high anyway, to increase even further. Low-budget accommodation of good quality is hard to find. To make up for the prices, standards are generally very high and there is a remarkably wide choice of luxury hotels: 50 hotels are ranked in the five-star category or even higher. All the well-known hotel chains are represented in Dubai. Moreover, there are some extraordinary gems of the hotel business that are unofficially classed as six-star houses for their quality and equipment. The Burj Al Arab was even awarded seven stars in Dubai. The luxury hotels of the Jumeirah Group, owned by the ruling family, also exceed the usual five-star grading in terms of their architecture and fittings.

At Christmas and Easter, at major Islamic holidays, for the Dubai Shopping Festival, special sporting events (golf, horse racing) and trade fairs many hotels are fully booked. Visitors may have to put up with disturbances caused by construction work, whether in the form of noise or the fact that cranes and half-built skyscrapers spoil the view.

During the summer months hotel prices fall by up to 60 per cent, as many hotels

Photo: Lobby in the Burj Al Arab

## Arabian nights: nowhere else in the world boasts such as wide selection of spectacular and luxurious hotels

are then half-empty. In the four weeks of Ramadan too, a period when hardly any Arab guests are travelling, the hotels have extremely attractive offers. Usually these are packages that include the breakfast buffet and an *ifthar dinner* (breaking fast in the evening).

Breakfast is often included in the room price, but usually 10 per cent service and 10 per cent tax have to be added.

Apartments and holiday houses are becoming more popular, especially with tourists who intend to spend more time in Dubai in the future to live and work. It is a useful way of getting to know life in the emirate outside the hotels. The apartment complexes of Golden Sands are not too expensive, and those who can afford it can also book luxury villas with a pool, for instance at *www.dubai-holiday-dreams.com*.

You will save money by booking a hotel in advance from home, either via the internet or through a travel agency. The *www.dubaitourism.ae* website lets you choose online from some 200 hotels.

Dubai's three youth hostels can also be booked online.

## HOTELS: EXPENSIVE

### THE ADDRESS DOWNTOWN DUBAI
(109 D4) (*∅ S5*)

This resort run by a chain opened in 2008. It tempts its guests with contemporary luxury, lifestyle and an impressive

### JEBEL ALI GOLF RESORT & SPA
(U B9) (*∅ B2*)

110 acres of gardens and park, lakes, splashing waterfalls, exotic plants from the Far East, its own 9-hole golf course and a big pool area create an oasis right by the sea with a private beach of white sand. The hotel has its own marina, jogging course and stables. The suites of the **INSIDER TIP** *Palm Tree Court* are accom-

Immodestly named hotel, not the worst place to stay in Dubai: The Address

site: directly opposite the Burj Khalifa at the heart of the new district called Downtown Dubai. Further selling points include an exquisite pool area 1000 m² in size and extra services such as checking in at the hotel's own airport lounge. If you stay here, book a ☀ room on the top floors of the 1004-ft building. *196 rooms | Burj Khalifa Boulevard | Downtown Dubai | tel. 04 4 36 88 88 | www.theaddress.com | Metro Red Line: Dubai Mall*

modated in separate villas with private access to the garden, and have their own reception and decoration in contemporary Balinese style. *260 rooms | Jebel Ali | tel. 04 8 83 60 00 | www.jebelali-interna tional.com | Metro Red Line: Jebel Ali*

### JUMEIRAH BEACH HOTEL
(106 C1) (*∅ N4*)

900 metres of private beach, almost two dozen restaurants and its own marina are just a few of the highlights of this hotel, which unofficially is a six-star address.

It is situated opposite the Burj Al Arab and next to the Wild Wadi aquapark. The building has a striking external appearance in the shape of a stylised wave. *598 rooms | Jumeirah Road | Jumeirah | tel. 04 3 48 00 00 | www.jumeirahbeach hotel.com | Metro Red Line: First Gulf Bank*

### THE PALACE ⚬⚬ (109 D4) (*🛈 S5*)

Opulence and tradition come together in this pleasantly low-rise hotel in the newly emerging in-location of Downtown Bur Dubai. The balconies of the rooms and suites (min. 51 m²) boast a view of the Burj Khalifa and Old Town. This is the right choice for guests who are attracted by luxury, Arabian atmosphere and closeness to the shopping malls: the Dubai Mall and Souk Al-Bahar are next door. *242 rooms | Burj Khalifa Boulevard | Downtown Dubai | tel. 04 4 28 78 88 | www.thepalace-dubai.com | Metro Red Line: Dubai Mall*

### PARK HYATT (110 C5) (*🛈 V6*)

The drive leading to the entrance of this luxury hotel passes through a landscaped park with grasses and palm trees right on the Dubai Creek. An Arabian and maritime mood with a hint of minimalism characterise the foyer and the rooms. It's only a few paces to the yachts on the Creek, and the golf course too is within teeing-off distance. In the restaurants the atmosphere makes you feel miles from the city bustle. The wonderful pool is shaded by dense palms, and the breakfast buffet is one of the best in Dubai. *225 rooms | Dubai Creek Golf & Yacht Club | Al-Garhoud | tel. 04 6 02 12 34 | www.dubai. park.hyatt.com | Metro Red Line: Deira City Centre*

### RAFFLES (110 B5) (*🛈 U6*)

One of the best city hotels: this pyramid-shaped 19-storey building next to the Wafi Mall has huge, luxurious rooms. In the glass tip of the tower, the ⚬⚬ *New Asia Bar* is an inviting place to have a drink with a panoramic view of the city. The spa lies in the middle of the extensive *Raffles Botanical Garden,* giving guests the impression that they are in the tropics. Ten restaurants and bars round off the facilities. *248 rooms | Sheikh Rashid Road | Wafi City | tel. 04 3 24 88 88 | www.raffles.com | Metro Green Line: Healthcare City*

### THE RITZ-CARLTON (104 B1) (*🛈 J3*)

A lot of people think this is still Dubai's finest beach hotel, because it is the most personal: with only six storeys and Mediterranean styling it resists the post-modern high-rise boom, forming a unique oasis with a private beach 300 m long. The lobby lounge has the atmosphere of an English club, especially when afternoon tea is being served. The hotel has superb gardens, an intimate Balinese spa, three pools, tennis courts, a gym and squash courts. A further advantage is its proximity to the Emirates Golf Club. To enjoy special luxury book one of the 50 Club rooms on the sixth floor with their own club restaurant, which spoils guests from breakfast time right through to the evening digestif. *138 rooms | Jumeirah Road | Jumeirah | tel. 04 3 99 40 00 | www.ritzcarlton.com | Metro Red Line: Dubai Marina*

### HOTELS: MODERATE

**INSIDER TIP** **ARABIAN COURTYARD**
(U B3) *(𝄢 V4)*

This large hotel complex is sited in the middle of the labyrinth of lanes of the Meena Bazar, opposite the Dubai Museum and at the heart of historic Dubai. The rooms are furnished in good quality, Arabian style. There is an outdoor pool, an oriental restaurant with plenty

# LUXURY HOTELS

### Burj Al Arab ★ (U D9) *(𝄢 N3)*

The spectacular façade of the 'Arabian Tower' shelters a sumptuous interior, a cross between Gianni Versace, Louis XIV and Walt Disney: gold leaf, velvet and brocade, crystal chandeliers, marble and granite. Even the smallest rooms are suites with a surface area of 170 m². *202 suites | Jumeirah Road | Umm Suqeim | tel. 04 3 01 77 77 | www.burj-al-arab.com | suite from 6000 Dh (through travel agents and online from 3500 Dh) | Metro Red Line: First Gulf Bank*

### Al-Qasr and Mina A'Salam (106 B1) *(𝄢 M4)*

The 'Palace' and the 'Haven of Peace' are the showcase parts of the Madinat Jumeirah luxury holiday complex. Crowned by wind towers, the hotels rise between man-made waterways. The rooms (minimum 55 m²) are furnished in opulent Arabian style. Boats transport guests to all places in the resort. *292 and 280 rooms | Jumeirah Road | Madinat Jumeirah | tel. 04 3 66 88 88 | www.madinatjumeirah.com | doubles from 2500 Dh | Metro Red Line: Sharaf*

### Al-Maha Desert Resort ★ (U C–D5) *(𝄢 O)*

This hotel complex in an 80 sq mile nature reserve for the oryx antelope places its guests in residences (min. 75 m²) with pools over which large Bedouin tents are spread. The price includes all meals, camel treks and riding Arab horses. *42 suites | Al-Maha Al-Ain Road (E66), turn-off 40 mi southeast of Dubai between Exit 50 (Margham) and Exit 51 (Muqab), then 6 mi on a track | tel. 04 3 03 42 22 | www.al-maha.com | suite from 5500 Dh*

### One&Only Royal Mirage ★ ● (U C9) *(𝄢 K3–Y4)*

Mosaics, marble, stucco and gold lend magnificence to the salons, and the rooms are furnished in a classy palace style. This complex consists of three hotels next to each other on the beach: *The Palace, Arabian Court* and *The Residence*. A hamam that's the stuff of dreams rounds off the luxury experience. *246 rooms | Al-Sufouh Road | Jumeirah | tel. 04 3 99 99 99 | www.oneandonlyresorts.com | doubles from 2500 Dh | Metro Red Line: Nakheel*

of character and the lovely Zaitoon Spa to pamper guests. *173 rooms | Al-Fahidi Street | Meena Bazar | Bur Dubai | tel. 04 3 519 111 | www.arabiancourtyard.com | Metro Green Line: Saeediya*

in several high-rise buildings. There are single-room studios (37 m²) and others with separate bedroom and living room (66 m²), **INSIDER TIP** suitable for four guests. The apartments have a fully

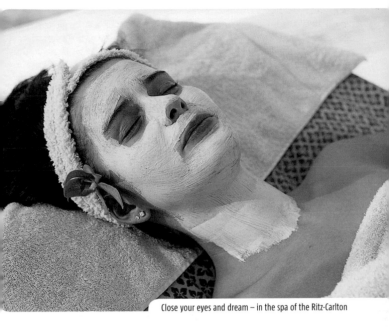

Close your eyes and dream – in the spa of the Ritz-Carlton

### FLORA GRAND HOTEL (111 D3) (*W5*)

A relatively old hotel with a modern glass facade and a small pool on the roof terrace. Well-kept rooms and suites with varied furnishings, several restaurants and a café. Free transfer service from the airport, daily shuttle to the malls, and lots of cheap restaurants nearby. *200 rooms | Al-Riqqa Street | Al-Riqqa | tel. 04 2 23 33 44 | www.florahotels.ae | Metro Red Line: Al Riqqa*

### GOLDEN SANDS 3 (110 B2) (*V4*)

Functional and modern without unnecessary luxuries. This is one of the city's largest apartment complexes, housed

equipped kitchenette and washing machine. Those who wish can have breakfast in the restaurant. Further amenities are a pool, gym, travel agency and car hire. Travel agents can book the apartments for you at a reasonable price. *269 apartments | Al-Mankhool Street (behind the Burjuman Centre) | Mankhool | tel. 04 3 55 55 53 | www.goldensandsdubai. com | Metro Red Line: Al-Karama*

### IBIS DEIRA CITY CENTRE
### (111 D5) (*W6*)

Attractively priced, new mid-range hotel with a pool, gym and bistro restaurant. A free shuttle to the airport is available,

Guests at the XVA Gallery enjoy individual surroundings

and there are many special offers. *365 rooms | 8th Street (opposite the Deira City Centre Mall) | Port Saeed | tel. 04 2 92 50 00 | www.ibishotel.com | Metro Red Line: Deira City Centre*

### K-PORTE (111 D3) ( *W5*)

Comfortable hotel with a free shuttle to the beach and airport, a rooftop pool, sauna, bars and restaurants, nightclub, garage. *117 rooms | corner of Al-Riqqa Street and Omar Bin al-Khattab Road | Al-Riqqa | tel. 04 2 24 34 33 | www.kporte. com | Metro Green Line and Red Line: Union Square*

### ORIENT GUEST HOUSE (U C3) (*V4*)

In the traditional Bastakiya quarter a historic two-storey building has been converted into an oriental-style guesthouse. Tastefully furnished rooms, some of them with rustic four-poster beds and Arabian furniture, are grouped around

a courtyard. *10 rooms | Sikka 15c | Al-Fahidi Street near R/A | Bur Dubai | tel. 04 3 51 91 11 | www.orientguesthouse.com | Metro Green Line: Saeediya*

### XVA GALLERY (U C3) (*V4*)

Oriental atmosphere and a great location in Bastakiya justify the somewhat higher prices of this boutique hotel. The rooms are on the small side, but were furnished in the Arabian style with antiques by a team of artists and interior designers to create a wonderful atmosphere. The building is a traditional wind tower house and keeps two beautiful courtyards for its guests. The hotel is run with a personal touch and has an art gallery and café attached. *7 rooms | Al-Fahidi Street at R/A (behind Sahary Gate and Basta Arts Café) | Bastakiya | tel. 04 3 53 53 83 | www.xvagallery.com | Metro Green Line: Saeediya*

## HOTEL: BUDGET

### ARABIAN PARK HOTEL
**(110 B5) (🗺 U6)**
Eight-storey building convenient for shopping near the Wafi City Mall (free shuttle bus); it has some larger rooms with balcony and a seawater pool. *318 rooms | Oud Metha Road 1 | Al-Jaddaf | tel. 04 3 24 59 99 | www.arabianparkhotel. com | Metro Green Line: Healthcare City*

### DOWNTOWN **(111 D2) (🗺 V4)**
Modernised hotel in the centre of Deira; the rooms have coffee and tea-making facilities. Laundry service, shuttle bus to the beach. *32 rooms | Nasser Square (behind the Sabkha bus station) | Deira | tel. 04 2 26 07 77 | www.downtownhotel dubai.com | Metro Green Line: Al Ras*

### MEENA PLAZA **(110 B2) (🗺 U4)**
Nine-storey 'Indian' hotel with a restaurant to match and two bars near the Burjuman Centre. There are smaller rooms but also 30 larger suites, all with a balcony, refrigerator, and TV. Ayurveda treatments, in-house coffee shop and free airport transfer. *82 rooms | Al-Mankhool Road (next to Choitrams) | Bur Dubai | tel. 04 3 514 2 22 | www. meenaplazahotel.20m.com | Metro Red Line: Al Karama*

### MIAMI **(111 D2) (🗺 W4)**
The cheap rooms are at the back, and the ones at the front with a balcony cost more; a few larger suites for families are also available. *44 rooms | Naif Road | Deira | tel. 04 2 29 53 35 | www.hotel miamidubai.com | Metro Green Line: Palm Deira*

### NOVA **(U B2) (🗺 V4)**
Situated in a lively area, and surrounded by restaurants and the shops of the Meena Bazaar. Basic rooms furnished to Indian standards, some of them with four beds. Internet access in the foyer. *84 rooms | Al-Fahidi Street | Meena Bazar | Bur Dubai | tel. 04 3 55 90 00 | www. dubainovahotel.com | Metro Green Line: Al Ghubaiba*

### SUN CITY **(U B3) (🗺 V4)**
Six-storey no-frills hotel near the Dubai Museum. It has a noisy Indian nightclub with live music, a coffee shop and an airport transfer service. Many of the guests are Asian. *66 rooms | Al-Fahidi Street/ Sikka 50A | Bur Dubai | tel. 04 3 53 68 88 | hsuncity@emirates.net.ae | Metro Green Line: Al Ghubaiba*

# LOW BUDGET

▶ The *Dubai Youth Hostel* has doubles and family rooms with bathroom, refrigerator and air-conditioning. The new extension has more comfort *(double 250 Dh)*, while the older part is cheaper. There is also a pool. *52 rooms | Al-Nahda Road 39, by the Al-Bustan Centre | Al-Qusais 1 | Al-Qusais* | **(120 C4) (🗺 Y6)** | *tel. 04 2 98 8151 | www.uaeyha.com*

▶ In the basic *Time Palace Hotel* near the Dubai Museum, the rooms have en-suite bathrooms and refrigerators. A double room with breakfast and airport transfer costs 360 Dh incl. tax and service. *55 rooms | Juma Masjid Street/Sikka 50A |* **(U B3) (🗺 V4)** *| Bur Dubai | tel. 04 3 53 2111 | www.time-palace.com | Metro Green Line: Saeediya*

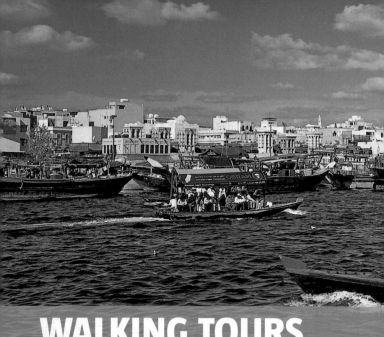
Photo: Dubai Creek

# WALKING TOURS

The tours are marked in green in the street atlas,
the pull-out map and on the back cover

## 1 FROM THE CREEK TO THE GOLD SOUK

Here you can breathe the air of Dubai's many worlds: for starters, old-fashioned wooden boats on Baniyas Road (Deira Corniche) with a backdrop of post-modern tower blocks. Then the route takes you through lively, noisy bazaar streets to the Gold Souk. Duration of the walk: 2–3 hours.

In Baniyas Road, one of the first streets built on the Creek in the Emirate of Dubai, you can get to know one more aspect of this multi-faceted city. While the continual process of change is apparent in this walk through the streets and the alleys branching off them, you can at the same time take a look behind the scenes and

immerse yourself in the world of small traders and craftsmen.

The route begins at the Sheraton Creek Hotel. Built right on the Creek in 1975, this was one of the city's first five-star hotels, but thanks to constant modernisation it seems in no way out of date. In the foyer you can sample its stylish luxury by lingering over a cup of tea in the lobby café.

After this take a stroll along the Creek, passing many dhows that are moored here. They are wooden Arabian boats that have been converted to floating restaurants. This might be a good opportunity to choose your ship and book an INSIDER TIP evening dinner cruise → p. 72. The eye-catching architecture on the other side of Baniyas Road is the glass office

## Wind tower houses, souks and an upmarket promenade: these walks show you many facets of Dubai old and new

block of Etisalat, the national telecommunications company: it has the shape of a gigantic mobile phone. The spherical telecommunications antenna on the roof reminds most observers of a huge golf ball, because after dark the sphere is illuminated by little lamps distributed across its surface in octagonal patterns. Dubai's city hall, the **Municipality Building**, has a top location with a view of the Creek and was designed in a striking post-modern style. An eight-storey square building clad in light-coloured marble surrounds a circular, hall-like building of red-brown granite. It is not really worth going inside. Water flows over an enormous marble sphere into a square basin. The chess-board pattern on the base of the stone dromedary that can be seen here is a reminder of the chess world championships that were held in Dubai more than two decades ago.

Traffic on the four-lane Baniyas Road, the Deira Corniche/Al-Khor Corniche, never diminishes day or night. Now the Creek is a very busy scene. In rows four

The ideal place for a break with a view: the Twin Towers, also known as the Rolex Towers

or five deep, heavily laden dhows lie by the quayside to be loaded or unloaded. Cars and trucks are parked on all sides, alongside towering heaps of goods and crates, car tyres and household wares. The destinations of the boats are Iran, Pakistan and the West Indies. The seamen live on the boats: they cook there, hang out their washing and play cards when they get a break.

Cross the road near to the main entrance of the **Radisson SAS Hotel**. Adjacent to the hotel lobby is an arcade with cafés, restaurants and shops. The cafés are frequented by business people and locals. Take a stroll along the shopping arcade:

you will see historic silver jewellery from Yemen and Asian art on display in the little antique shops. When you leave the hotel at the other end you pass from its air-conditioned interior with the soothing strains of classical music into the noise of traffic and the humid heat of the city.

The **Twin Towers**, locally known as the Rolex Towers, rear up in front of you. The little shopping complex is not particularly interesting, but on the third floor several restaurants and a food court with ⚓ a big outdoor terrace is the ideal spot for enjoying the view of the Creek. After it goes dark, INSIDER TIP▶ try smoking a hubble-bubble (shisha) on the balcony – a service that is explicitly offered to women, too, including those travelling alone. From here it is a few hundred metres to the **Deira Old Souk Abra Station**. An underpass beneath Baniyas Road leads from the Creek to **Old Baladiya Street**. On a small open space here there are a few little sales points including a juice bar that squeezes fruit fresh on the spot. This is an oasis of old-style oriental trading. Spices are sold from open jute sacks, there is a whiff of incense in the air and sometimes Arabian music emanates from a cassette recorder. Take the opportunity here to stock up on little water bottles (2 Dh).

Stroll further along Old Baladiya Street until you reach Sikkat al-Khail Street on the right and the entrance to the covered **Gold Souk** → p. 34 and 65. For many years road traffic has been banned from this paved street, which is roofed with wooden pergolas to provide shade. During the day the rows of shops lined up side by side look somewhat abandoned, as this lane doesn't get crowded until the evening – which means that the traders take all the more interest in customers who turn up in daylight hours. They untiringly answer questions about prices and place the items that you ask about on the scales. If you show interest in spending any considerable sum, the staff will eagerly offer tea and cola. Customers in the lanes of the souk get friendly and courteous treatment, even if they are just asking about the price.

Sikkat al-Khail Street leads to the **Perfume Souk** → p. 65; here you can take in the heady scents of hundreds of different oils, essences of incense and joss sticks, and of course this is a good chance for you to take a whiff of the orient back home with you.

Now heading back in a westerly direction you pass the **Spice Souk** → p. 36 and 65; and here too there are seductive aromas in the air. Indian and Pakistani traders sell cardamom, cinnamon, nuts, saffron, henna powder and much more from open jute sacks. Incense is offered in various qualities, as are exotic perfumed oils, joss sticks, baskets and ceramic goods.

Beyond Old Baladiya Street lies Al-Ras Road; on the street parallel to it to the north, Al-Ahmadiya Street, you will find the city's oldest school: the **Al-Ahmadiya School** → p. 32. Next door, the **Heritage House** → p. 34 is worth seeing, and both buildings are a must when visiting the historical sights of Dubai.

Returning now to Old Baladiya Street you come to the Creek at the Deira Old Souk Abra Station.

## 2 FROM THE HERITAGE VILLAGE TO BASTAKIYA

**After taking a look at 'Dubai 100 years ago' you wander across to the old fort and pass the wind tower houses of the traditional Bastakiya quarter. The tour can last between 2 and 4 hours, depending on what interests you, There are several ways to get to the start of this walk, the Shindagha waterfront of Bur Dubai: take a taxi from Deira through the road tunnel, walk through the pedestrian tunnel or – the most pleasant alternative – take an abra boat from Deira across to Bur Dubai.**

Begin on the waterfront path along the Creek in front of the **Heritage & Diving Village** → p. 30, where the history of the emirate is kept alive. Several popular restaurants have set up tables right by the water on the promenade. You might want to take a pit stop at the **Kan Zaman Restaurant and Café** → p. 57 and spend some time watching the boats on the

Creek or looking across to the Deira side with its ultra-modern high-rises.

Next stop is the **Sheikh Saeed al-Maktoum House** → p. 31, the perfectly restored former palace of Dubai's ruling family. Strolling further along the bank of the Creek, you'll see Arabs, Asians and westerners queuing at the **Bur Dubai Abra Station**. There are always lots of little boats waiting at the jetties before they cross over to the other side. This is a bustling spot that smells of diesel oil – and has the thoroughly oriental atmosphere that is getting harder and harder to find in Dubai.

Above the boat dock, towards the city, is part of the **Textile Souk** → p. 65 (also known as the Bur Dubai Souk). Here In-dian traders sell fabrics by the metre. In tailors' shops clothes such as jackets and skirts INSIDER TIP are made to specifications, and trousers, jackets and suits for men and women are made to measure. The path leads past the abra dock to the historic commercial building of **Bayt al-Wakeel** → p. 29 and 57, which lies right on the Creek. It was built in 1934, the first administrative building in Dubai. The INSIDER TIP wooden terrace is a magnet for tourists who want to sniff the air of old Dubai.

For the host of Indian and Pakistani men who live in low-grade rented accommodation in Bur Dubai the refreshments on offer here have become too expensive. On their days off and in the evenings

What would a holiday in Dubai be without a shopping trip? Here Bur Dubai Souk

the men sit together in groups in open spaces by the Creek, on the ground and in the entrances to buildings, converse and watch the passers-by.

Parallel to the Creek runs the covered **Bur Dubai Souk**. Its wares, above all Dubai T-shirts, fabrics and pashmina scarves, as well as souvenirs, are mainly bought by tourists, but also by many of the Asian guest workers.

Pass the Old Souk Abra Station to reach the **Grand Mosque** → p. 30, which is situated between the Creek and the fort, and is visible from afar thanks to its great domes. You can also reach the mosque via Bin-Talib Street, which goes past the Textile Souk. Non-Muslims are not allowed into the mosque, but can come here at prayer times to see how men with head coverings or caps come from all points of the compass and stream into the mosque to pray. Their faces and clothing reveal that they come from Muslim countries in Asia.

On the side of the Grand Mosque that faces away from the Creek you will come to the historic **Al-Fahidi Fort**, now home to the **Dubai Museum** → p. 30, the largest and most important museum in the city. Closer to the Creek is the **Ruler's Court**, a government building of the ruling family in Islamic architectural style. Continue along the Creek or Al-Fahidi Street to **Bastakiya** → p. 28, the historic quarter between Al-Fahidi Roundabout and the Creek. Many of the buildings here have wind towers and are built of coral stone and mud bricks. Today, they house museums, cafés and galleries. In the narrow alleyways here it's possible to walk around without being bothered by cars, which are ever-present in Dubai. When you are ready for a break there is nowhere better than the **Basta Arts Café** → p. 50.

## THE WALK: STROLL, SHOP AND ENJOY

**The latest thing among European expatriates is a stroll** through the new Dubai between Jumeirah Beach and Dubai Marina: from the Ritz-Carlton Hotel to the Sheraton Jumeirah Beach, staying on the exclusively designed seafront promenade called **The Walk.**

This is where it's at for those who like people-watching, shopping, and indulging themselves. It is a rendezvous for joggers and health-conscious hedonists. Just over a mile long and partly paved with cobblestones, the path is lined by palm trees and other tropical plants. It belongs to the new **Dubai Marina** city district. Many restaurants and cafés with outdoor tables are on The Walk, as are the Oasis Beach Tower Hotel, the Hilton Jumeirah Resort and the **Jumeirah Beach Residences**, which is why it's also known as JBR Walk. In several places steps lead up to the Beach Residences, 36 massive apartment towers run by the Jumeirah company, and to several hotels. In between there are more open spaces adorned with fountains and lots of greenery, supermarkets, shops and small shopping arcades that are worth looking at.

Dubai residents like to order a latte macchiato or a vanilla-flavoured ice coffee at **Il Caffe di Roma** *(tel. 04 4 37 02 28 | www.Ilcaffediroma.com | Moderate).* For vegetarians the ⚜ **The Indian Pavilion** *(tel. 04 4 37 02 33 | Moderate)* is a must, not least for its location above the JBR Walk with a terrace, canvas sun canopy – and a view. Amongst all the shops and boutiques, Saks Fifth Avenue and the London label Aiyana (bags and luxurious accessories) are the ones that people flock to here.

# TRAVEL WITH KIDS

In the summer months fun for children is mainly confined to activities in air-conditioned rooms, as it is much too hot even for aquaparks and the beach. From October to April however Dubai is a destination that children and teenagers love. If you are looking for a hotel with its own beach for a small child, the only options are the expensive hotels on Jumeirah Beach. Like other 5-star and some 4-star hotels they have superbly equipped children's clubs.

### AQUAVENTURE ⭐ (U C8) (𝄢 L2)

The water chutes in the huge aquapark of the Atlantis Resort (free of charge for hotel guests) are more than just a way to cool off. Seven of them begin at the 30 m-high 'Ziggurat' tower, a real adventure for older children and teenagers. *Daily 9am–6pm | Atlantis Resort | Crescent Road/Jumeirah Road | The Palm Jumeirah | www.atlantisthepalm.com | admission 285 Dh, children (up to 1.20 m in height) 220 Dh | Metro Red Line: Nakheel*

### DUBAI AQUARIUM & UNDERWATER ZOO ⭐ (109 D4) (𝄢 S5)

Fascinating: watch over 30,000 marine animals, including 400 sharks and rays in ● Dubai's aquarium with its 33 by 8 m viewing window. Visitors walk through a glass tunnel, surrounded by fluorescent jellyfish, sea anemones and many rare fish. In the Underwater Zoo on the second floor you will find exhibitions and smaller aquariums, for example with fish otters and seals. *Sun–Wed 10am–10pm, Thu–Sat 10am–midnight | Dubai Mall | Sheikh Zayed Road | www.thedubai aquarium.com | free admission, tunnel and zoo 50 Dh | Metro Red Line: Dubai Mall*

### DUBAI AUTODROME (U C10) (𝄢 K–L 8)

After three trial circuits with the driving teacher (20 min, i.e. 10–15 rounds cost 750–875 Dh depending on the vehicle), kids can have fun on the 1200 m track with 17 curves, a tunnel and a bridge, in two categories of vehicles: one for 7- to 12-year-olds and another for older kids. *Sun–Wed 10am–10pm, Thu–Sat 11–1am | Emirates Road, E311 (Sheikh Zayed Road, 4th Interchange, exit 39 towards Barsha) | Motor City | www.dubaiautodrome.com | 15 min 100 Dh | Metro Red Line: Mall of the Emirates*

### INSIDER TIP DUBAI ICE RINK
### (109 D4) (𝄢 S5)

Enormous ice rink on the ground floor of the Dubai Mall. As the hall is cooled only to 20 °C/68 °F, a pullover or jacket is all that's needed. *Daily 11.15am–1.15pm,*

## Beaches, water parks and fascinating underwater worlds: Dubai offers children lots of attractions

*1.30–3.30 pm, 5–7pm, 7.30–9.30pm, 9.45–11.45pm | Dubai Mall | Sheikh Zayed Road, 1st Interchange, Doha Street | www.dubaiicerink.com | 2 hours 50 Dh (incl. skates) | Metro Red Line: Dubai Mall*

### KIDZANIA (109 D4) (*💷 S5*)
Where children can play at being adults in an adult world: drive cars, take off in a plane, be a doctor or salesperson – lots of fun but taken seriously here. *Sun–Wed 9am–10pm, Thu–Sat 9am–midnight | Dubai Mall | www.kidzania.ae | admission 90 Dh | children up to 16 years 125 Dh | Metro Red Line: Dubai Mall*

### SHOPPING WITH CHILDREN
In Dubai's shopping malls children and teenagers will discover their favourite brands. In most malls there are *amusement parks* with bowling alleys, dodgems and the like. One of the best equipped is *Magic Planet* in the *Mall of the Emirates* (U D9) (*💷 M5*) (*Metro Red Line: Mall of the Emirates*) which boasts a climbing wall.

### STARGATE (110 A3–4) (*💷 U5*)
This three-storey indoor theme park has not only the usual attractions (3D cinema, ice rink, go-karts, dodgems) but also a roller coaster that starts at the dome of the building and takes you outside! *Sat–Wed 10am–10pm, Thu/Fri 11am–11pm | Gate 4, Area A, Zabeel Park | www.stargatedubai.com | admission Zabeel Park 5 Dh, chip card for recharging: 2 Dh, extra charges depending on the attraction 10–25 Dh for children | Metro Red Line: Jafilia*

### WILD WADI WATER PARK
(U D9) (*💷 N4*)
Fourteen of the park's thirty water chutes are connected to each other. The one called Jumeirah Sceirah drops 27 m at a speed of 80 km/h, and in the Tunnel of Doom it gets dark. *Daily 11am–7pm, Nov–Jan until 6pm | Jumeirah Road (in front of the Burj Al Arab) | www.wildwadi.com | admission 195 Dh, children (up to 1.10 m in height) 165 Dh | Metro Red Line: First Gulf Bank*

# FESTIVALS & EVENTS

Festivals and public holidays mainly follow the Islamic calendar. The Islamic calendar begins on 15 July 622, i.e. 2012 is therefore the year 1433 A.H. (Anno Hejra) by this system. Friday is the weekly day of rest, and the weekend includes Saturday.

## HOLIDAYS

**Hejra** New Year (15 Nov 2012, 4 Nov 2013, 24 Oct 2014); **Maulid al-Nabi** Birthday of the Prophet Mohammed (4 Feb 2012, 24 Jan 2013, 13 Jan 2014); **6 Aug** Accession Day in the UAE, the day when President Sheikh Zayed took up office; **Lailat al-Miraj** Ascension of the Prophet Mohammed (16 June 2012, 5 June 2013, 25 May 2014); **2 Dec** National Day in the Emirates, day of the unification of the seven emirates to become the UAE in 1971; **25 Dec** Christmas

## MOVABLE HOLIDAYS

### EID AL-ADHA
is the name of the three-day festival of sacrifice at the end of the ten-day period of pilgrimage *(hadj)* to Mecca. The Koran prescribes that all Muslims should make a pilgrimage to Mecca once in their lifetime, unless they are unable to do so for health or financial reasons. Muslims slaughter a sheep and invite their relatives (26–29 Oct 2012, 15–18 Oct 2013, 4–7 Oct 2014).

### RAMADAN
The holy month for Muslims is a period of fasting and prayer. From sunrise to sunset they are not allowed to eat, drink, smoke or pursue pleasure (20 July to 18 Aug 2012, 9 July–7 Aug 2013, 29 June–27 July 2014).

### EID AL-FITR
The three-day festival for breaking the fast at the end of Ramadan is celebrated with banquets – in hotels too – and the exchange of presents when visiting relatives; people put on their best clothes; in the cities there are fireworks, fairs and folk dances (19–21 Aug 2012, 8–10 Aug 2013, 28–30 July 2014).

## EVENTS

### JANUARY
Professional golfers arrive for the ▶ *Dubai Desert Classic golf tournament*, part of the European PGA Tour *(end of Jan/early Feb | www.dubaidesertclassic.com)*.

## Desert Rock & Desert Classics:
Dubai hosts high-calibre events, concerts with world stars and famous sporting contests

### JANUARY/FEBRUARY

▶ ★ ● *Dubai Shopping Festival:* this 30-day shopping festival is the ultimate spree. The shops (some 30,000) offer discounts of between 20 and 70 per cent, and the whole city is decked out to create a festival atmosphere. Fairy lights, fireworks and countless free events every day attract more than 3 million visitors from all around the world. As several big sporting events take place at this time of the year, it is advisable to book a hotel months in advance. Emirates Airlines allows passengers INSIDER TIP 10 kg of additional free baggage during the festival. *www.mydsf.com*

### FEBRUARY

The ▶ *Dubai Tennis Championships* pull in the tennis fans *(2nd half of the month | www.barclaysdubaitennischampionships.com).*

### MARCH

For the ▶ INSIDER TIP *Desert Rock Festival* international rock and pop stars come to the emirate *(beginning of the month | www.cmsme.com).*
The ▶ *Dubai World Cup* boasts the world's biggest prize money for a horse race *(a week at the end of the month | www.dubaiworldcup.com).*

### OCTOBER TO APRIL

In the winter season, ▶ horse *and camel races* take place in Dubai at weekends. INSIDER TIP *Camel races* are held Thu–Sat from 2.30pm; spectators are also welcome to watch the training from 7.30 am. Locals and expatriates from all around the world come to the horse races: Thu/Fri evening (see p. 70).

### 2 DECEMBER

▶ *National Day:* the day of the foundation of the United Arab Emirates is celebrated with many events (folklore, boat races etc.).

# LINKS, BLOGS, APPS & MORE

LINKS

▶ www.conciergedubai.com The online version of this high-class magazine for visitors has recommendations for hotels and upmarket shopping

▶ www.dubaicityguide.com Where to go: restaurants, bars, shopping and events listings

▶ www.dubaiculture.ae An excellent source for the cultural life of the city, from museums to the Gulf Film Festival

▶ www.uaeinteract.com The website of the Ministry of Information and Culture has lots of current news about politics and business, but also tourism-related information

▶ www.arabianwildlife.com Videos, images and information about flora and fauna, especially birds

BLOGS & FORUMS

▶ www.secretdubai.blogspot.com Uninhibited blogging about all sorts of subjects by the people who live there

▶ www.dubai-videos.com Short films about buildings, hotels, streets, and life on the street and in Dubai

▶ www.tripadvisor.co.uk If you click on 'Forums', 'Middle East' and 'United Arab Emirates', you have the opportunity to put questions about Dubai and read what others are writing

Regardless of whether you are still preparing your trip or already in Dubai: these addresses will provide you with more information, videos and networks to make your holiday even more enjoyable

▶ www.dubai-video.com 23-minute film of a helicopter flight over Dubai – the highlights from the air are Burj Al Arab, The Palm Jumeirah and mega-projects under construction

▶ www.dubaitourism.ae The official tourist website includes videos about Dubai in its media database, including on spas and shopping

▶ Definitely Dubai iPhone app produced by Dubai Tourism with a city guide and information about events and special offers

▶ Shopping Guide Tips and addresses for department stores, bookshops, art & antiques, electronic goods and fashion for iPhone

▶ Around Me Programme by Tweakersoft that informs you about the place you are currently in: cafés, restaurants, cinema, hotels etc., with city plan and distances

▶ www.dubaitourism.ae You can download an interactive city plan by clicking 'Trade Resources'

▶ Go Dubai City map of Dubai plus events and activities for iPhone

▶ twitter.com/Hallodubai Up-to-the-minute news from the expatriate scene

▶ www.facebook.com/dubaionline More news and exchanges amongst Dubai residents

▶ http://wiki.couchsurfing.org/en/Dubai A wiki with practical information by the couchsurfing network, which brings together people in different countries. If you would like to get to know or stay with people in Dubai, you need to register under www.couchsurfing.org

# TRAVEL TIPS

## ARRIVAL

✈ *Emirates (www.emirates.com)* flies daily from London Heathrow, British Airways (www.britishairways.com) twice daily. Emirates has a non-stop service to Dubai from New York. Other direct flights from Britain to Dubai are operated by Virgin Atlantic (*www.virgin-atlantic.com*), Gulf Air (*www.gulfair.com*) and Etihad Airways (London and Manchester; *www.etihadairways.com*). Qatar Airways flies direct from London and Manchester. You can also fly with Kuwait Airways (*www.kuwait-airways.com*), Gulf Air, Qatar Airways (*www.qatarairways.com*), Oman Air (*www.omanair.com*) or Etihad (*www.etihadairways.com*) and combine a trip to Dubai with a stay in Kuwait, Bahrain, Qatar, Muscat or Abu Dhabi. The budget airline Fly Dubai (*www.flydubai.com*) has low-price connections between Dubai and Bahrain, Qatar, Kuwait and Muscat. A flight from London Heathrow to Dubai lasts seven hours.

## RESPONSIBLE TRAVEL

It doesn't take a lot to be environmentally friendly whilst travelling. Don't just think about your carbon footprint whilst flying to and from your holiday destination but also about how you can protect nature and culture abroad. As a tourist it is especially important to respect nature, look out for local products, cycle instead of driving, save water and much more. If you would like to find out more about eco-tourism please visit: *www.ecotourism.org*

## BANKS & MONEY

You can change quickly and without restrictions from money changers, usually at a favourable rate. In banks it takes longer, and the hotels give an unfavourable rate of exchange. Cash points (ATMs) can be found everywhere, and credit cards are widely accepted.

## BUSES

### CITY BUSES
Dubai has many bus routes *(www.rta.ae)*, which are mainly used by Asian workers. A journey costs 1.5–2.5 Dh. Bus 401 goes from the airport to the hotels in Deira, bus 402 to Bur Dubai *(both routes 3 Dh)*. From the Deira bus station there are connections to the Jubail bus station in the centre of Sharjah *(5 Dh)*.

### OVERLAND BUSES
*Emirates Express* connects Dubai (stops in Deira and Bur Dubai) with Abu Dhabi and Hatta every hour, with Muscat (Oman) and Fujairah 4 times daily, with Al-Ain 6 times daily; fares are 15–40 Dh.

### WATERBUS
Ten air-conditioned boats carrying 35 passengers run on four routes on the western Creek between Deira (Sabkha, Beniyas) and Bur Dubai (Shindagha, Al-Seef Road). *Daily 6–11pm | 4 Dh per trip.* A tourist version of the waterbus covers the full distance between Shindagha and Creek Park *(25 Dh)*.

# From arrival to weather

**From the start to the end of the holiday: useful addresses and information for your trip to Dubai**

## CARS & CAR HIRE

Traffic congestion is bad in Dubai and parking is often a problem. As taxis are cheap, there is no point in using a hire car in the city. To hire (from 150 Dh per day) you need a national driving licence, for a trip to Oman an international licence. It is usually cheaper to book a car before you leave home.

Petrol is cheap, the highways wide and well signposted. Max. speed 120 km/h, in built-up areas 50 or 60 km/h. In case of an accident, you must wait for the police to arrive. The alcohol limit for drivers is zero!

## CITY TOURS

A semi-open-top *double-decker bus* leaves the Wafi Centre and Deira City Centre every hour to tour the main sights of Bur Dubai and Deira. There are two routes and a total of 20 stops where passengers can hop on and off. The price includes a dhow trip on the Creek, a guided walk in Bur Dubai and free admission to the Dubai Museum and the Sheikh Saeed al-Maktoum House. A two-hour night tour is also on offer. *The Big Bus | May–Sept daily 3–8pm, Oct–April daily 9am–6pm, every 30 mins | 200 Dh, children up to 15 years of age 100 Dh, family (2+2) 500 Dh | www.bigbustours.com*

The *Wonderbus,* an amphibian vehicle that moves on land and water, leaves from the Burjuman shopping complex in Mankhool daily at 1pm and 5pm. After exploring the city it goes down to the Creek for a water tour. *Duration 1.5 hours | 125 Dh, children up to 12 years of age 85 Dh, family (2+2) 390 Dh | www.wonderbusdubai.com*

## CLIMATE & WHEN TO GO

In summer it is hot and humid on the coast (around 40 °C/105°F), and dry in the interior. The best time for travelling is therefore winter: between October and April. In that period the climate is mild with lots of sunshine and daytime top temperatures between 25 and 35 °C/75–95°F, at night 17–20 °C/63–68°F.

## CLOTHING

Even in winter, the weather is very warm, and summer clothes are adequate. However, in the chilly air-conditioning of hotels, restaurants and shopping malls you will need a pullover or a jacket. The etiquette of the Arab world forbids short trousers, naked shoulders and for women anything that is short, tight-fitting or see-through. A light scarf to cover head, shoulders or arms is therefore an essential item.

## CONSULATES & EMBASSIES

### UAE EMBASSY IN UK (ALSO SERVING IRISH CITIZENS)
30 Princes Gate | London SW7 1PT | tel. 020 7581 1281 | www.uaeembassyuk.net

### UAE EMBASSY IN USA
3522 International Court | NW Suite #400 | Washington, DC 20008 | tel. 202 243 2400 | www.uae-embassy.org

### UAE EMBASSY IN CANADA
125 Boteler Street | | Ottawa K1N 0A4 | tel. 613 565 7272 | www.uae-embassy.ae/ca/

## BRITISH EMBASSY IN DUBAI

Al Seef Road / P.O. Box 65 / Tel. 04 309 4444 | *http://ukinuae.fco.gov.uk*. Irish citizens should contact the Irish Embassy of Ireland in Saudi Arabia: Diplomatic Quarter / P.O. Box 94349 / Riyadh 11693 / tel. 966 1 488 2300 / www.embassy ofireland.org.sa

## USA EMBASSY IN DUBAI

Corner of Al Seef Road and Sheikh Khalifa bin Zayed Rd Road / P.O. Box 121777 / tel. 971-4-309-4000 / http://dubai.usconsu late.gov

## CONSULATE GENERAL OF CANADA

Bank St. Building, 7th floor, Khalid bin Waleed St. (behind Burjuman Shopping Centre)/ P.O. Box 52472 / P.O. Box 121777 / tel. 971-4-314-5555 / dubai@ international.gc.ca

### CUSTOMS

800 cigarettes and 2 litres of alcohol may be imported to Dubai. For those returning to the EU the limits are 200 cigarettes, 1 litre of spirits, other goods to a value of £ 390 *(see www.hmrc.gov. uk/customs)*; to the USA normally goods to a value of US$ 800 including 2 litres of alcoholic drinks; see *www.cbp.gov* for all details.

### ELECTRICITY

220–240 V, 50 Hertz; most sockets are the English type with three pins.

### EMERGENCY SERVICES

Police *tel. 999 and tel. 8 00 44 38 (English)*
Ambulance, emergency doctor *tel. 998 and tel. 999*
Fire brigade *tel. 997*

### HEALTH

No vaccinations are required, but protection against tetanus, polio and hepatitis A is advisable. The risk of malaria applies only to distant wadis with stagnant water. Hygienic conditions are excellent, even in basic restaurants, but as you may be unaccustomed to some of the food, consider taking something for digestive problems. The standard of medical care in Dubai is excellent. Most doctors are not locals and speak English. There is an American hospital *(American Hospital Dubai | Karama | tel. 04 336 77 77 | www. ahdubai.com)*. Emergency treatment is free of charge in state hospitals.

### IMMIGRATION

On arrival at the airport in Dubai (and in Abu Dhabi) you are given a *Visa on Arrival*. It is free of charge and valid for 30 days. Your passport has to be valid for 6 months. There are no border controls between the different emirates.

# BUDGETING

| | | |
|---|---|---|
| Coffee | 10 Dh/15 Dh | |
| | *in a food court/café* | |
| Beer | 20–30 Dh | |
| | *for a bottle* | |
| Snack | 7.50–12.50 Dh | |
| | *for a shawarma (flatbread with meat)* | |
| Petrol | 1.50 Dh | |
| | *for 1 litre* | |
| Souvenir | from 35 Dh | |
| | *for a cotton pashmina scarf* | |
| Gold | approx. 100 Dh | |
| | *for 1 gram, 22 carat* | |

## INFORMATION

**DUBAI DEPARTMENT OF TOURISM AND COMMERCE MARKETING**

*For UK and Ireland: Nuffield House | 41–46 Piccadilly | London W1J 0DS | tel. 020 7321 6110 | www.dubaitourism.ae*
*For USA and Canada: 25 West 45th Street | Suite #405 | New York | NY 10036 | tel : 001 212 575 2262 |*
*In Dubai: P. O. Box 594 | Dubai | UAE | tel. 971 4 2 23 00 00*

Welcome kiosks in the airport (24 hrs), on Baniyas Square (9am–11pm), in the shopping malls Deira City, Burjuman, Hamanrain, Wafi and Mercato (all 10am–10pm) and in the National Bank of Dubai (NBD) Building, Baniyas Road, 10th floor.

### CITY MAGAZINES AND LISTINGS

– What's On, monthly, 10 Dh, *www.whatsonlive.com*
– TimeOut Dubai, weekly, 7 Dh, *www.timeoutdubai.com*
– Concierge Dubai, monthly, free, *www.conciergedubai.com*
– Discover Dubai, monthly, free, with coupons for restaurants, travel agents and other services
– City info, monthly, free, *www.explocity.com*

## METRO

The trains of the *Dubai Light Rail Transit System (LRT)* runs on an ● elevated track 4 m high and in a tunnel in the city centre. The first line entered operation in 2009, but not all stations of the *Red Line and Green Line* are in use yet. The ticket price consists of a once-only basic cost for a magnetic card of 2 Dh and then up to 4 Dh per single journey, depending on the zones. Passengers can store credit on the chip card and use them for journeys. A *Day Pass* for an unlimited number of journeys costs 14 Dh. On Fridays the Metro runs only after 2pm.

## OPENING TIMES

Banks: *Sun–Thu 8am–1pm*; authorities: *Sun–Thu 7.30am–2.30pm*; shopping malls: *Sat–Thu 10am–10pm, Fri 2–10pm*; shops: *Sat–Thu 9am–1pm and 4–8pm*

## PERSONAL SAFETY

Dubai is a very safe place, where fraud and harassment are unusual. *Dubai Tourism and Commerce Marketing* has a dedicated telephone number, free of charge, for tourists wishing to make a complaint: *tel. 8 00 70 90.*

# CURRENCY CONVERTER

| £ | Dh | Dh | £ |
|---|---|---|---|
| 1 | 5.80 | 1 | 0.17 |
| 3 | 17.40 | 3 | 0.51 |
| 5 | 29 | 5 | 0.86 |
| 13 | 75.40 | 13 | 2.24 |
| 40 | 232 | 40 | 6.90 |
| 75 | 435 | 75 | 12.90 |
| 120 | 696 | 120 | 20.70 |
| 250 | 1,450 | 250 | 43 |
| 500 | 2,900 | 500 | 86 |

| $ | Dh | Dh | $ |
|---|---|---|---|
| 1 | 3.70 | 1 | 0.27 |
| 3 | 11 | 3 | 0.82 |
| 5 | 18.30 | 5 | 1.36 |
| 13 | 47.75 | 13 | 3.54 |
| 40 | 147 | 40 | 10.90 |
| 75 | 275 | 75 | 20 |
| 120 | 440 | 120 | 33 |
| 250 | 918 | 250 | 68 |
| 500 | 1,836 | 500 | 136 |

For current exchange rates see www.xe.com

## PHONE & MOBILE PHONE

The country code for Dubai from Europe is *00971 4,* from Dubai to the UK *0044,* to Ireland 00353, to the USA and Canada *001.* Local landline calls are free. With a phone card you can call direct all over the world from a phone booth.

The mobile network in Dubai is GSM, and the national phone company is *Etisalat (tel. 04 101 | www.etisalat.co.ae).* European mobile phones work in Dubai. To avoid paying high roaming charges it is worth considering buying a pre-paid SIM card from Etisalat, so that charges for incoming calls are not made. Text messaging is cheap. Using your mailbox can be expensive, so it may be worth switching off before you leave.

## PHOTOGRAPHY

Do not take photos of people without getting their permission first. For religious reasons it is not permitted to photograph Muslim girls and women. Military installations, police stations, harbours and airstrips are also out of bounds for photographers; at the rulers' palaces it is best to ask the guards first before you reach for your camera.

# WEATHER IN DUBAI

| | Jan | Feb | March | April | May | June | July | Aug | Sept | Oct | Nov | Dec |
|---|---|---|---|---|---|---|---|---|---|---|---|---|
| Daytime temperatures in °C/°F | 20/68 | 21/70 | 24/75 | 28/82 | 33/91 | 35/95 | 37/99 | 38/100 | 36/97 | 32/90 | 27/81 | 22/72 |
| Nighttime temperatures in °C/°F | 14/57 | 15/59 | 17/63 | 21/70 | 26/79 | 28/82 | 29/84 | 30/86 | 27/81 | 24/75 | 21/70 | 16/61 |
| Sunshine hours/day | 8 | 8 | 8 | 10 | 12 | 12 | 10 | 10 | 10 | 10 | 9 | 8 |
| Precipitation days/month | 1 | 2 | 1 | 2 | 0 | 0 | 0 | 0 | 0 | 0 | 1 | 1 |
| Water temperature in °C/°F | 19/66 | 18/64 | 23/73 | 27/81 | 27/81 | 27/81 | 29/84 | 32/90 | 27/81 | 27/81 | 25/77 | 24/75 |

## POST

There are post offices in all parts of the city. A postcard to Europe costs 3 Dh and takes a week; expect a few days more for North America.

## PRICES & CURRENCY

The currency used in the UAE is the *Dirham (Dh or AED)*, divided into 100 *fils*. Dubai is not a cheap country for travellers, and hotels are particularly expensive.

## TAXI

For taxis the basic charge is 3 Dh (3.50 Dh on Fri/Sat and from 10pm; 25 Dh from the airport; 6 Dh if you call the taxi to the hotel) plus 1.60 Dh per kilometre. At tolls (Maktoum Bridge, Garhoud Bridge, Sheikh Zayed Road) the fare increases by 4 Dh; the minimum fare is 10 Dh. Taxis have yellow number plates. In Dubai there are also taxis for women, recognisable by the pink roof and pink interior (and by the fact that the driver is a woman). At malls shoppers often have to queue for a taxi.

## TIME

GMT plus 4 hours (in summer BST plus 3 hours).

## TIPPING

In restaurants it is usual to give 10 per cent if you are satisfied and no *service charge* was included on the bill. In taxis tips are not expected, but round up the amount. Porters get 5 Dh, chambermaids 5 Dh per night.

## TRANSCRIPTION

Transcription of Arabian words using the Latin alphabet is done in different ways, depending on what people hear: Jazeera, Jazirah. MARCO POLO uses the version employed locally and corresponding generally to an English style of spelling. This is

Part of the programme on all city tours: Bur Khalifa, the world's tallest building

the version seen in Dubai on public signs, which use both Latin and Arabic script.

## WOMEN TRAVELLING SOLO

This is not a problem in Dubai – providing you observe the usual rules of behaviour there. Don't flirt openly with Muslim men, and that includes looking into their eyes! Scanty clothing is also to be avoided, except at beach hotels and beach clubs.

# NOTES

## MARCO POLO TRAVEL GUIDES

ALGARVE
AMSTERDAM
BARCELONA
BERLIN
BUDAPEST
CORFU
DUBROVNIK & DAL-
  MATIAN COAST
DUBAI
EDINBURGH
FINLAND
FLORENCE
FLORIDA
FRENCH RIVIERA
  NICE, CANNES &
  MONACO

IRELAND
KOS
LAKE GARDA
LANZAROTE
LONDON
MADEIRA
  PORTO SANTO
MALLORCA
MALTA
  GOZO
NEW YORK

NORWAY
PARIS
RHODES
ROME
SAN FRANCISCO
STOCKHOLM
THAILAND
VENICE

MARCO POLO
With ROAD ATLAS & PULL-OUT MAP
LAKE GARDA
E BALDO WITH MOUNTAIN BIKE
in Malcesine takes bikes too
SSES" IN SALÒ
cate "Dacetti"
Travel with Insider Tips

MARCO POLO
With STREET ATLAS & PULL-OUT MAP
NEW YORK
OWS, WILD FLOWERS AND SKYSCRAPERS
ic: the High Line in Chelsea
IL ON CLOUD NINE
top bar at 230 Fifth Street
Travel with Insider Tips

MARCO POLO
With ROAD ATLAS & PULL-OUT MAP
FRENCH RIVIERA
NICE, CANNES & MONACO
SPECTACULAR GRAND CANYON DU VERDON
Breath-taking scenery that takes some beating
SNIFFING THE AIR
The perfume manufacturers of Grasse
Travel with Insider Tips
www.marcopolouk.com

MARCO POLO
With STREET ATLAS & PULL-OUT MAP
BERLIN
A STUNNING ISLAND JUST FOR ART
Showcasing treasures from around the world
STAY COOL AT NIGHT
scene sets the trend
Travel with Insider Tips

MARCO POLO
With ROAD ATLAS & PULL-OUT MAP
ALLORCA
AN FLAIR IN THE MEDITERRANEAN
allorca's most beautiful beach
E ..IN" CROWD MEET
Fonda in Deià
Travel with Insider Tips

- PACKED WITH INSIDER TIPS
- BEST WALKS AND TOURS
- FULL-COLOUR PULL-OUT MAP
  AND STREET ATLAS

www.marcopolouk.com

# STREET ATLAS

The green line ████ indicates the Walking tours

All tours are also marked on the pull-out map

Photo: Shaik Zayed Road

# Exploring Dubai

The map on the back cover shows how the area has been sub-divided

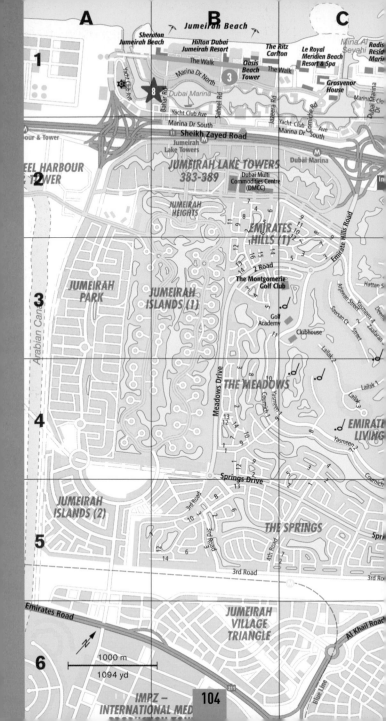

# A

**1**

Yacht Club Ave
⊕
Bahar Rd
★ **8**
Dubai Marina
Yacht Club Ave

ur & Tower

⚓EL HARBOUR
T♦ WER

**2**

Arabian Canal

JUMEIRAH
PARK

**3**

**4**

JUMEIRAH
ISLANDS (2)

**5**

Emirates Road

1000 m
1094 yd

**6**

# B

Jumeirah Beach

**Sheraton
Jumeirah Beach**
**Hilton Dubai
Jumeirah Resort**
The Walk
Marina Dr North
**3**
Oasis
Beach
Tower
Jaheel Rd

Marina Dr South
Sheikh Zayed Road
Jumeirah
Lake Towers

JUMEIRAH LAKE TOWERS
*383–389*
Dubai Multi
Commodities Centre
(DMCC)

JUMEIRAH
HEIGHTS

7
6
9
11
EMIRATES
HILLS (1)
12
1
10
12
13
15
14
16
2 Road

**The Montgomerie
Golf Club**

JUMEIRAH
ISLANDS (1)

Golf
Academy

Meadows Drive

10
THE MEADOWS
Yasmeen 1
Courtich 1
13
12
1
9
10
1
12

Springs Drive
13

3rd Road
8
10
2

3rd Road

THE SPRINGS

12
14
6

3rd Road

JUMEIRAH
VILLAGE
TRIANGLE

IMPZ –
INTERNATIONAL MED

# C

The Ritz
Carlton
Le Royal
Meridien Beach
Resort & Spa
Mina Al
Seyahi
Radis
Resid
Marin

The Walk
**Grosvenor
House**
Jazeera Rd
Marina Clo
Corniche Rd
Yacht Club
Ave
Marina Dr
South

Dubai Marina

Emirate Hills Road

Hattan S

Athenan Street
Vaimeen 4
Zaafaran
Saysan Ct
Street

Clubhouse

Lailak 2
Lailak 1
Lailak 3

EMIRATE
LIVING

Yasmeen
Yasmeen
2

Courtich

Spr
Spr

3rd Ro

Al Khail Road
Blue Line

**104**

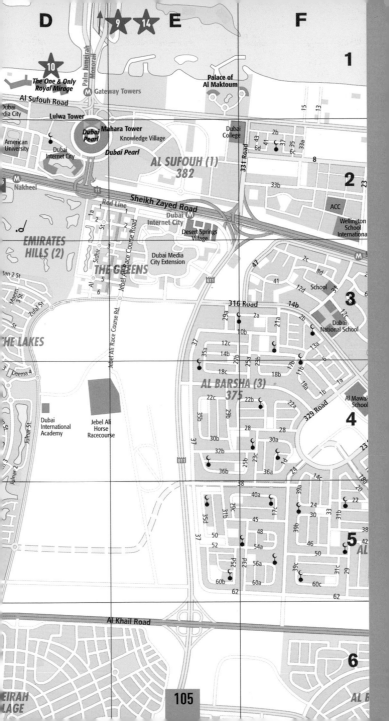

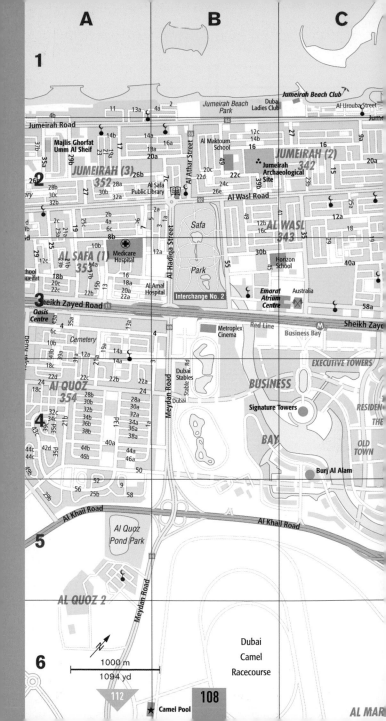

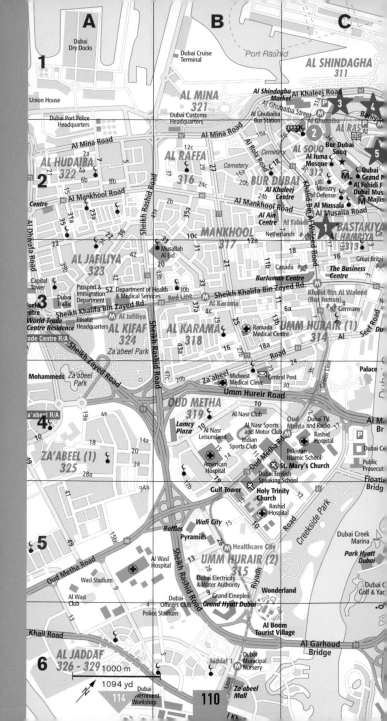

**A**

1

Dubai
Dry Docks

Union House

Dubai Port Police
Headquarters

**AL HUDAIBA**
**322**

2
4a
6b    8b

*Centre*

Al Mankhool Road

35  31a  23a

22  36

42

**AL JAFILIYA**
**323**
39b

Capital
Tower
World
Centre
**3**
Dubai
Traffic

Passport &
Immigration
Department

**World Trade**
**Centre Residence**

*Al Dhiyafa Road*

**Sheikh Zayed Road**

Mohammeds
Za'abeel
Park

Za'abeel R/A
**4**
10   19a   4a
18   20
19   24
28a

**ZA'ABEEL (1)**
**325**

41   34a

49   15b   66

Oud Metha Road

Al Wasl
Club

Wasl Stadium

Khail Road

**AL JADDAF**
**326 - 329**  1000 m

1094 yd

114

Dubai
Government
Workshop

**B**

Dubai Cruise
Terminal

**AL MINA**
**321**
Dubai Customs
Headquarters

Al Mina Road

12c

**AL RAFFA**
**316**   27

16a   20b
24c
2b

24b

**MANKHOOL**
**317**

10c

Musallah
Al Eid

20

43b

Department of Health
& Medical Services   30b

Red Line

Elisalat
Headquarters

**AL JAFILIYA**

Za'abeel Park

**AL KIFAF**
**324**

43a

47c   20b

Za'abeel
Park

**OUD METHA**
**319**

Lomcy
Plaza

Al Nasr
Leisureland

Al Nasr Club

Al Nasr Sports
and Motor Club
Indian
Sports Club

American
Hospital

5   14

12b

**Gulf Tower**

**Wafi City**

**Raffles**
**Pyramids**

26

**UMM HURAIR (2)**
**315**

Al Wasl
Hospital

13

28

**Healthcare City**

Dubai Electricity
& Water Authority

**Grand Cineplex**
**Grand Hyatt Dubai**

Dubai
Officers Club
Police Stadium

Jaddaf 1

Za'abeel
Mall

**110**

**C**

**AL SHINDAGHA**
**311**

Al Shindagha
Market   Al Khaleej Road

Al Ghubaiba Street
Al Ghubaiba
Bus Station

Al Ghubaiba

**AL SOUQ**   Bur Dubai
Al Juma   Souq
Mosque

**AL RAS**

**5**
Dubai
**Grand M**
Al Fahidi F
Dubai Mus
Majlis

**312**

M

Ministry
of Defense

Al Mussala

**BUR DUBAI**

**Al Khaleej**
**Centre**

Al Mankhool Road

**Al Ain**
**Centre**

Al Fahidi

Netherlands

Burjuman Centre

Sheikh Khalifa Bin Zayed Rd.

Canada   **The Business**
**Centre**

Khalid Bin Al Waleed
(Bur Juman)   8

Germany

Al Musalla Road

**BASTAKIYA**
**AL HAMRIYA**
**313**

Great Britai

16

18

11b

M  Al Karama

6a

**UMM HURAIR (1)**
**314**

Al

Ramada
Medical Centre

25

16   27b   18a

M
Al Jafiliya

**AL KARAMA**
**318**

4c

9

77

Midwest
Medical Clinic

Central Post

30

Umm Hureir Road

10

Al Nasr Club

Oud   Dubai TV.
Metha   and Radio

Rashid
Hospital

Pakistan
Islamic School
**St. Mary's Church**

Dubai English
Speaking School

**Holy Trinity**
**Church**

Rashid
Hospital

**Creekside Park**

Palace

Al M
Br

Dubai Ce

Dubai
Prosecut

Floatin
Bridge

Dubai Creek
Marina

**Park Hyatt**
**Dubai**

Park Hyatt
Dubai

Dubai
Golf & Yac

Wonderland

Riyadh

**Al Boom**
**Tourist Village**

Al Garhoud
Bridge

Dubai
Municipal
Nursery

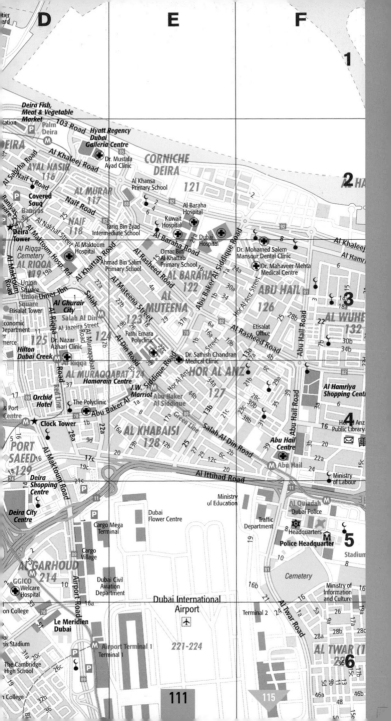

**D**   **E**   **F**

**1**

**2**

Deira Fish,
Meat & Vegetable
Market
103 Road   Hyatt Regency
Palm   Dubai
Deira   Galleria Centre

DEIRA   Al Khaleej Road

Dr. Mustafa
Ayad Clinic   CORNICHE
DEIRA

AYAL NASIR   Al Khansa
116   Primary School   121

Covered   AL MURAR
Souq   117   Al Baraha
Naif Road   Hospital

NAIF   Kuwait
118   Hospital   Al Baraha Road

Deira   Tariq Bin Zyad   Dubai
Tower   Intermediate School   Hospital   Dr. Mohamed Salem
Mansour Dental Clinic

Al Riqqa   Al Maktoum   Omar Bin
Cemetery   Hospital   Ahmad Bin Salim   Al Khattab   Dr. Mahaveer Mehta
AL RIQQA   Primary School   Primary School   Medical Centre
119   AL BARAHA
Union   122   ABU HAIL
Square   126
Umer Ibn   AL MUTEENA   Etisalat
Etisalat Tower   Al Ghurair   123   Office   AL WUHE
City   Al Jazeera Street   Al Rasheed Road   132
Hilton   125   Salah Al Din   124   Al Matena Street
Dubai Creek   Dr. Nazar   Fathi Emara
Azhari Clinic   Polyclinic   Dr. Sathish Chandran
Riqqa   Medical Clinic

AL MURAQQABAT 124   HOR AL ANZ
Hamarain Centre   127   Al Hamriya
Shopping Centr
Orchid   J.W.
Hotel   The Polyclinic   Marriot   Abu Baker Al
Abu Baker   Siddique   Hor
Clock Tower   AL KHABAISI   Salah Al Din Road   Public Library
128   Abu Hail
PORT   Centre   Ministry
SAEED   Al Maktoum Road   Al Ittihad Road   of Labour
129
Deira   Ministry
Shopping   Dubai   of Education
Centre   Flower Centre   Al Qiadah
Dubai Police
Deira City   Cargo Mega   Traffic
Centre   Terminal   Department   Headquarters
Police Headquarter
Cargo   Stadium
Village
AL GARHOUD   Cemetery
GGICO 214   Dubai Civil
Welcare   Aviation   Ministry of
Hospital   Department   Information
and Culture
Dubai International   Terminal 2
Le Meridien   Airport
Dubai   AL TWAR (1
Airport Terminal 1   221-224
Terminal 1
The Cambridge
High School

**111**   **115**

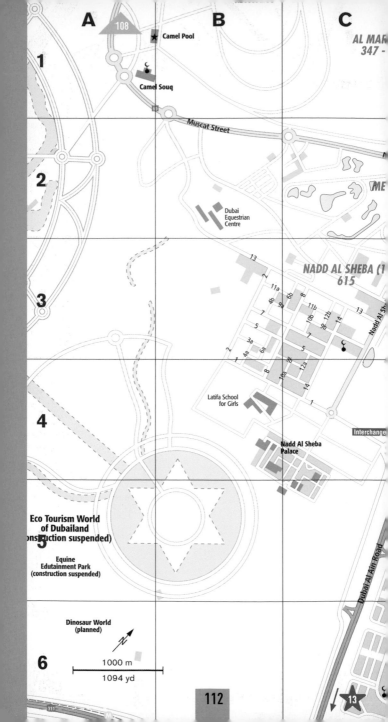

# A

108

★ Camel Pool

♙ Camel Souq

# B

Muscat Street

Dubai
Equestrian
Centre

13
2
11a 6b 8
4b 9a 11b
7 10b 12b 13
5 9b 14
3a 6a 7
2 4a 5
1 3b 12a
8 10a 14
Latifa School
for Girls 1

Nadd Al Sheba
Palace

# C

AL MAR
347 –

ME

*NADD AL SHEBA (1*
*615*

Naddi Al Sh–

Interchange

Eco Tourism World
of Dubailand
(construction suspended)

Equine
Edutainment Park
(construction suspended)

Dinosaur World
(planned)

N

1000 m
1094 yd

Dubai Al Ain Road

# 1

# 2

# 3

# 4

# 5

# 6

↓ 13

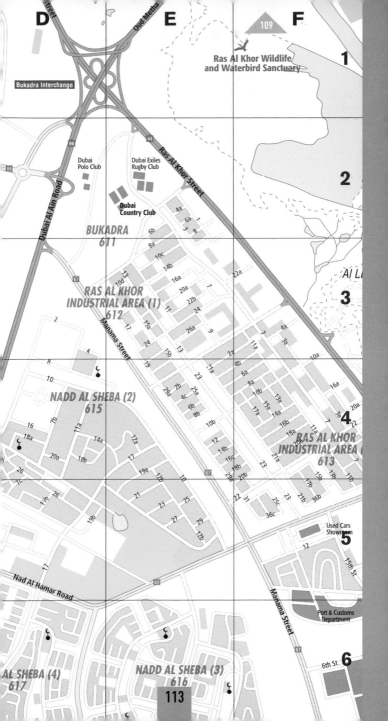

**1**

109

Ras Al Khor Wildlife
and Waterbird Sanctuary

Bukadra Interchange

**2**

Dubai Al Ain Road

Dubai
Polo Club

Dubai Exiles
Rugby Club

Ras Al Khor Street

Dubai
Country Club

**BUKADRA**
**611**

Al L

**3**

**RAS AL KHOR**
**INDUSTRIAL AREA (1)**
**612**

Manama Street

**NADD AL SHEBA (2)**
**615**

**RAS AL KHOR**
**INDUSTRIAL AREA (**
**613**

**4**

Used Cars
Showroom

**5**

15th St

Nad Al Hamar Road

Manama Street

Port & Customs
Department

**6**

6th St

**AL SHEBA (4)**
**617**

**NADD AL SHEBA (3)**
**616**

113

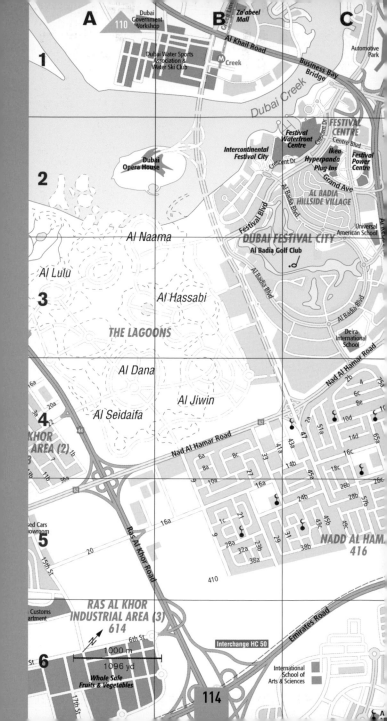

**A** · **B** · **C**

110

Dubai Government Workshop

Za'abeel Mall

Al Khail Road

Green Line

**1**

Dubai Water Sports Association & Water Ski Club

Creek

Business Bay Bridge

Automotive Park

Dubai Creek

**2**

Dubai Opera House

Festival Waterfront Centre

Intercontinental Festival City

FESTIVAL CENTRE

Centre Blvd

Ikea
Hyperpanda
Plug-Ins

Festival Power Centre

Crescent Dr

Crescent Dr

Grand Ave

AL BADIA HILLSIDE VILLAGE

Festival Blvd

Al Badia Blvd

Al Naama

Universal American School

DUBAI FESTIVAL CITY

Al Badia Golf Club

Al Lulu

**3**

Al Hassabi

THE LAGOONS

Al Badia Blvd

Al Badia Blvd

Deira International School

Nad Al Hamar Road

2b

Al Dana

4

6c
8e

Al Jiwin

75a

Al Seidaifa

2a

10d

10

**4**

KHOR AREA (2)

6a

20a

3a

44

Nad Al Hamar Road

47

51a

14d

65a

3a

7

1b

6a

8c

33

43a

45a

16c

18c

26c

11b

36a

8a

27

14b

62

9

10a

16a

24b

26b

28b

57b

1c

21

45b

49c

**5**

Used Cars Showroom

16a

9

28a

32a

23b

29

31

38b

43c

NADD AL HAM.
416

15th St

20

410

RAS AL KHOR INDUSTRIAL AREA (3)
614

Customs Department

6th St

1000 m

1096 yd

Emirates Road

Interchange HC 50

**6**

17th St

Whole Sale Fruits & Vegetables

St

International School of Arts & Sciences

114

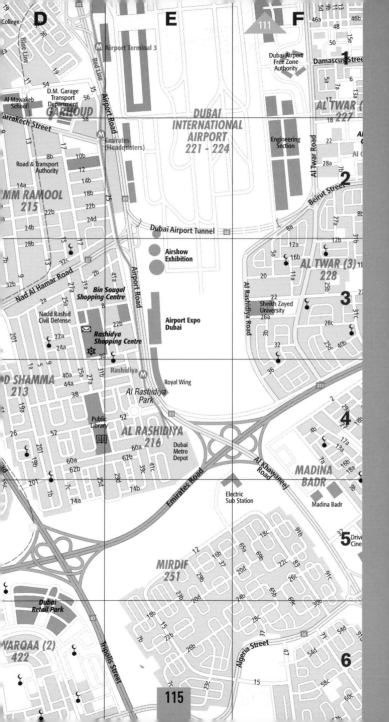

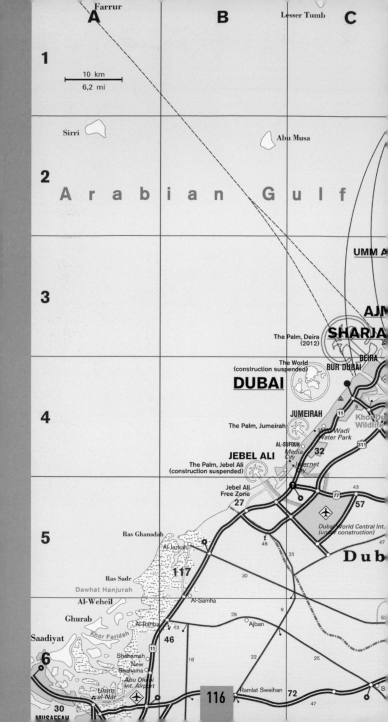

Farrur

A   B   Lesser Tumb   C

1

10 km
6,2 mi

Sirri

Abu Musa

2   A r a b i a n   G u l f

UMM A

3   AJM

The Palm, Deira
(2012)   SHARJA

DEIRA

The World
(construction suspended)   BUR DUBAI

DUBAI

4   JUMEIRAH   11   Khor Du
Wildlife

The Palm, Jumeirah   Wild Wadi
Water Park

AL-SUFOUH   311

Media
City   32

JEBEL ALI   Internet
City

The Palm, Jebel Ali
(construction suspended)

Jebel Ali
Free Zone   43

27   77   57

Dubai World Central Int.
(under construction)   47

5   Ras Ghanadah   1
46

Al Jazirah   23   D u b

30

Ras Sadr   117

Dawhat Hanjurah

Al-Weheil   Al-Samha

Ghurab   29   9
Ajban   55

Saadiyat   Al-Rahba   13

Khor Faridah   46   25

18   22

Shahamah
New
Shahama   11   72
Abu Dhabi   Ramlat Sweihan
Int. Airport

Umm   116
al-Nar

6

30   47

MUSAFFAH

This index contains a selection of the streets and squares shown on the street atlas

# STREET INDEX

# KEY TO STREET ATLAS

M̂ ☷ Museum, Bühne
Museum, Stage

ℹ Information
Information

☾ ✝ Moschee, Kirche
Mosque, Church

⊕ ✲ Krankenhaus, Polizei
Hospital, Police

✉ 🚋 Post, Busbahnhof
Post, Bus terminal

♟ ★ Denkmal, Sehenswürdigkeit
Monument, Point of interest

🏰 🏰 Burg, -ruine
Castle, -ruin

∴ 🏌 Archäologische Stätte, Golfplatz
Archaeological site, Golf course

P P Parkplatz, Parkhaus
Parking, Car park

⚔ Konsulat, Botschaft
Consulate, Embassy

⛵ Jachthafen
Marina

🏖 Strand
Beach

✈ Internationaler Flughafen
International airport

✈ Nationaler Flughafen
National airport

—Ⓜ— U-Bahn
Metro

— — Fähre
Ferry

▪ Bemerkenswertes Gebäude
Notable building

▪ Öffentliches Gebäude
Public building

▫ Grünfläche
Green

☐ Unbebaute Fläche
Space

▬ Stadtspaziergänge
Walking tours

★15 MARCO POLO Highlight
MARCO POLO Highlight

# INDEX

All the places, islands and destinations for trips mentioned in the book are listed in this index. Bold figures refer to the main entry.

# WRITE TO US

e-mail: info@marcopologuides.co.uk

Did you have a great holiday?
Is there something on your mind?
Whatever it is, let us know!
Whether you want to praise, alert us
to errors or give us a personal tip –
MARCO POLO would be pleased to
hear from you.
We do everything we can to provide
the very latest information for your trip.

Nevertheless, despite all of our authors'
thorough research, errors can creep
in. MARCO POLO does not accept any
liability for this. Please contact us by
e-mail or post.

MARCO POLO Travel Publishing Ltd
Pinewood, Chineham Business Park
Crockford Lane, Chineham
Basingstoke, Hampshire RG24 8AL
United Kingdom

**PICTURE CREDITS**
Cover Photograph: Dubai Marina, waterway with boats, Getty Images/Photographer's Choice: Fraser Hall
Photos: The Address Hotels + Resorts (16 bottom); Dubai Fashion Week (17 top); R. Freyer (36, 40, 82/83, 86);
Getty Images/Photographer's Choice: F. Hall (1 top); centre Forst-Gill (94 top); R. M. Gill (9, 24 r., 30, 47, 71,
88, 88/89, 94 bottom), The Holistic Institute: Robeya (17 bottom); Huber: Schmid (flap l., 3 centre , 3 bottom,
18/19, 65, 66/67, 68, 74/75); iStockphoto.com: Flavia Bottazzini (16 centre ); The Jam Jar LLC (16 top); centre
Kirchgessner (89); Laif: Brunner (20), Ebert (12/13), Heuer (79), Kirchgessner (2 centre top, 7), Krause (34, 91);
mauritius images: Alamy (flap r., 2 top, 3 top, 4, 5, 8, 10/11, 15, 23, 25, 39, 42/43, 44/45, 50, 56 r., 58/59, 63,
76, 84, 90, 90/91, 95, 101), Axiom Photographic (106/107), Mirau (2 centre bottom, 26/27); mauritius images/
imagebroker: Tack (6); D. Renckhoff (2 bottom, 24 l., 32, 33, 48/49, 53, 55, 56 l., 57, 60, 72, 80); M. Wöbcke
(1 bottom)

**1st Edition 2012**
Worldwide Distribution: Marco Polo Travel Publishing Ltd, Pinewood, Chineham Business Park,
Crockford Lane, Basingstoke, Hampshire RG24 8AL, United Kingdom. Email: sales@marcopolouk.com
© MAIRDUMONT GmbH & Co. KG, Ostfildern
Chief editors: Michaela Lienemann (concept, managing editor), Marion Zorn (concept, text editor)
Author: Manfred Wöbcke; Editor: Petra Klose
Programme supervision: Ann-Katrin Kutzner, Nikolai Michaelis, Silwen Randebrock
Picture editor: Gabriele Forst
What's hot: wunder media, Munich;
Cartography road atlas: DuMont Reisekartografie, Fürstenfeldbruck; © MAIRDUMONT, Ostfildern
Cartography pull-out map: DuMont Reisekartografie, Fürstenfeldbruck; © MAIRDUMONT, Ostfildern
Design: milchhof : atelier, Berlin; Front cover, pull-out map cover, page 1: factor product munich
Translated from German by John Sykes, Cologne; editor of the English edition: Kathleen Becker, Lisbon
All rights reserved. No part of this book may be reproduced, stored in a retrieval system or transmitted in any
form or by any means (electronic, mechanical, photocopying, recording or otherwise) without prior written
permission from the publisher.
Printed in Germany on non-chlorine bleached paper.

# DOS & DON'TS ☝

Some things are best avoided in Dubai

## DRINKING TOO MUCH ALCOHOL

In Dubai you can be served any drink you want in several restaurants and in the hotels. Enjoy it, but take care: anyone who is obviously drunk can expect to be arrested and imprisoned.

## APPROACHING ARAB WOMEN

Many Arab women do not want to be approached by foreigners, even for asking directions, or to have their photo taken. When greeting Arab women it is not customary to shake their hand.

## WADI BASHING

Tours through the desert and into the wadis by 4WD vehicles destroy the plants that grow laboriously on this barren soil under the blazing sun. A favourite bit of fun on these expeditions is to drive through watercourses and watering holes. This is very bad for the environment – and unfortunately the Emiratis don't set a good example.

## WEARING UNSUITABLE CLOTHING

In Dubai it is prohibited to leave the beach and the pool area wearing your swimming things. If you appear in public naked or topless, you can expect to pay a fine or even go to jail. Even when taking a walk or going on an excursion, you should make sure legs and arms are covered up. Bear in mind that the way of life is different in Islamic countries.

## DRIVING INTO THE DESERT ALONE

If you have a hire car that's not a 4 x 4, resist the temptation to leave the road and drive into the desert. The sand may be flat and look as if it's hard, but the unpractised eye fails to see the soft patches, and all of a sudden, you're stuck.

## TRAVEL DURING RAMADAN

During the annual fast for the month of Ramadan, public life in Dubai is very restricted. Shops and restaurants don't open until after dark, the hotel lobby is empty, and it's hard to find a taxi. Food and drink are only available after dusk – or from the room service.

## EXPLORE DUBAI IN A HIRE CAR

New roads are being built all the time, and buildings, hotels and whole residential quarters shoot up in no time at all. This means that drivers in Dubai spend a lot of time in traffic hold-ups. If you plan to stay in the city, do without a hire car and take taxis instead. They can be found everywhere and are not expensive.

## IMPORT OR TAKE DRUGS

Importing drugs to Dubai or taking them is a very risky business. Even an extremely small quantity of hashish will put you behind bars if you are caught.